# The Sierra Club Guide to Safe Drinking Water

# The Sierra Club Guide to Safe Drinking Water

*by Scott Alan Lewis*

*Afterword by Carl Pope,*
*Executive Director, Sierra Club*

**Sierra Club Books**
**San Francisco**

The Sierra Club, founded in 1892 by John Muir, has devoted itself to the study and protection of the earth's scenic and ecological resources—mountains, wetlands, woodlands, wild shores and rivers, deserts and plains. The publishing program of the Sierra Club offers books to the public as a nonprofit educational service in the hope that they may enlarge the public's understanding of the Club's basic concerns. The point of view expressed in each book, however, does not necessarily represent that of the Club. The Sierra Club has some sixty chapters coast to coast, in Canada, Hawaii, and Alaska. For information about how you may participate in its programs to preserve wilderness and the quality of life, please address inquiries to Sierra Club, 730 Polk Street, San Francisco, CA 94109.

Library of Congress Cataloging-in-Publication Data

Lewis, Scott, 1959–
    The Sierra Club guide to safe drinking water / by Scott Alan Lewis.
        p.    cm.
    Includes bibliographical references (p. 93).
    ISBN 0-87156-355-X (alk. paper)
    1. Drinking water—Health aspects—United States.  2. Drinking water—contamination—United States.  3. Drinking water—Purification—United States.  4. Drinking water—Government policy—United States.  I. Sierra Club.
RA592.A1L48  1996
363.6'1—dc20                                                    95-38942
                                                                      CIP

Production by Janet Vail
Cover design by Paula Schlosser
Book design by Susan Colen/Park Press

Printed in the United States of America on acid-free paper containing a minimum of 50% recovered waste paper, of which at least 10% of the fiber content is post-consumer waste

10 9 8 7 6 5 4 3 2 1

# Contents

**Acknowledgments**  **ix**

**Preface**  **xi**
 The Drinking Water Crisis

**1 Drinking Water Contaminants from A to Z**  **1**
 What's in the Water Besides Water  1
 Pathogens  2
 Inorganic Chemicals and Metals  7
 Synthetic Organic Chemicals (SOCs)  15
 Radioactive Materials  18
 Additives  20

**2 The Broken Promise of Pure Water**  **24**
 The Safe Drinking Water Act  24
 Clean Water: Possibilities and Realities  29
 If the Answers Are So Easy, Why Is There a Problem?  33

**3 What's in YOUR Drinking Water?**  **35**

**4 The City List**  **40**

**5 Home Treatment Systems for Unsafe Water**  **51**
 Purifying Your Own  52
 A Consumer's Guide to Water Purifiers  54
 The Most Comprehensive Filters  56
 The Second Most Comprehensive Filters  57
 Less Comprehensive Filters  59

**6 Buying Safe Water**  **68**
 Vendor Water  68
 Bottled Water  69

**7  Change the World**                                        **80**
Specific Steps to Improve Our Drinking Water        81

**Epilogue**                                                   **87**
Water of Life                                                  87

**Afterword, by Carl Pope**                                    **90**

**Suggested Reading**                                          **93**

**Appendix A**                                                 **95**
EPA Drinking Water Standards

**Appendix B**                                                 **103**
State Water Agencies

**Appendix C**                                                 **109**
EPA Regional Offices

**Appendix D**                                                 **111**
Water Purification Equipment Manufacturers

*For Zachary, Emily, Julian, Emmet, Spencer, and Mariah. May we leave for you a better world than we have found.*

## Acknowledgments

My first thanks go to Barbara Ras of Sierra Club Books for being the catalyst behind this project, and to Erik Migdail, my editor. I am also grateful for the assistance of Alex Levinson and Katherine Hohmann of the Sierra Club, and for providing materials, Nancy Culotta of NSF International and Brian Cohen of the Environmental Working Group. For soul support and general inspiration, accolades of adoration to my amazing wife, Laura.

Finally, for indispensable guidance and advice, I must thank Natural Resources Defense Council Senior Attorney Erik Olson, without a doubt one of the country's outstanding advocates for clean drinking water.

# The Drinking Water Crisis

*Summary*

**T**urn on the faucet and fill a glass with cool, clear water. As you take a drink, imagine the rain clouds and rivers, waterfalls and subterranean streams carrying water on its endless course through the world around us and bringing that water to you.

Rising from ocean to sky, forming clouds, then raining back down to the earth, trickling and flowing in rivulets, in rivers, and even underground, water moves in a vast, immeasurable circle as broad as the earth and sky. As it washes and flows across the land, down mountainside and over city street, draining both farmland and your own backyard or neighborhood park, water bears with it the story of where it has been.

Minerals essential to our health dissolve in groundwater and surface streams, enriching the water we drink, while agricultural pesticides and toxic factory discharges pour into rivers and lakes, killing fish and wildlife, and collecting in human tissue. More than any other feature of the environment, water connects and binds us with the world around us.

Throughout the history of human civilization, the presence of clean drinking water has played an instrumental role in determining where people chose to settle and how villages, towns, and cities grew. The United States has an abundant fresh water supply, but the pressures of economic development and population growth strain the quality and the quantity of water available for drinking. Four trillion gallons of rain fall on the United States every day, filling rivers and lakes and percolating through the soil to recharge immense underground reservoirs called aquifers. Each day, homeowners, factories, industrial users, and agricultural irri-

## Water Facts

- Each day, enough rain falls on the United States to cover the entire state of Vermont with 2 feet of water.
- Each day, U.S. water users withdraw enough water to fill a line of Olympic-size swimming pools that would reach around the world.
- Water makes up a full 70 percent of your body mass.

gators withdraw 300 billion gallons from this water supply, using water for everything from washing the car and watering the lawn to cooling the reactor cores of nuclear power plants. Sooner or later, most of the water taken out of the system finds a path back into a river, lake, or groundwater supply, along with whatever contaminants it has picked up along the way.

Making sure that the water you drink is pure is one of the most important steps you can take to protect your health and the health of your family. But you cannot always tell about the quality of your water just by looking at it—water can look clear in a glass and still contain toxic chemicals or bacterial and viral pathogens that can make you sick.

For example, in April 1993 a microscopic organism called *Cryptosporidium* caused more than 400,000 illnesses in Milwaukee, Wisconsin, and left 100 people dead. Among those killed were Sandra Leverance, a forty-one-year-old mother of two children, ages thirteen and ten, and Sophia Rudek, a woman in her sixties. In the spring of 1994, two more outbreaks of the same parasite killed nineteen and sickened more than 100 in Las Vegas and forced Milwaukee again to warn its households not to drink the water. Ironically, just the day before the second outbreak in Milwaukee, the U.S. Senate had voted to weaken the Safe Drinking Water Act, the federal law governing drinking water purity, even though more than 180,000 violations of the act were reported in 1993 and 1994 alone, affecting 92 million people.

To purify their water, larger cities and towns use centralized treatment plants and a variety of technologies ranging from simple screens, sand filtration, and chlorination to complex mechanical and chemical systems. When these methods fail, water customers are left vulnerable to a variety of chemical and biological hazards. Although large water systems supply the majority of the U.S. population, 80 percent of the water delivery systems in this country have fewer than 3,000 customers, and together serve 20 million Americans. These small systems often cannot afford to pay for the necessary tests and equipment to ensure safe water to their customers, and can be exempted from federal standards by demonstrating economic hardship. This leaves customers at risk.

To respond to the drinking water crisis, an entire industry has emerged to test water quality and provide individuals, families, and institutions with pure and safe drinking water, with options ranging from home filtration and purification to bottled water and purified water delivered by truck. This book will explain how you can find out what is in your water, and will explore the advantages and disadvantages of the various alternatives to drinking tap water. Chapter 1 describes many of the most common contaminants found in drinking water supplies throughout the country. Chapter 3 will help you get information about the quality of your water, and Chapters 5 and 6 will help you make sure the water you drink is healthy and safe.

Finally, communities have begun to realize that protecting drinking water from contamination can often be more effective than trying to remove pollution once it is in the water. This, however, is complicated by the fact that drinking water supplies often originate in river valleys, watersheds, and underground pools distant from the point of use. For example, New York City provides 1.5 billion gallons of water a day to 9 million people through a complex of dams, underground tunnels, and aqueducts, delivering its supply from the Catskill Mountains, 100 miles away. But because removing contaminants once they are in the water generally costs more and is less reliable than preventing pollution in the first place, cities have begun to take action to protect their water at the source. Chapter 7 discusses how you can support these efforts in your town.

There is a drinking water crisis in the United States today. The majority of American homes, apartment buildings, schools, hospitals, and offices rely on a water supply that is inherently unsafe. As a first step, we must protect our health and safety by making sure the water we drink is safe. At the same time, we must insist on a water delivery system that ensures all communities a safe, healthy drinking water supply. This book is a call to action, designed to help you achieve both of these goals.

**1**

○

# Drinking Water Contaminants from A to Z

The water flowing from your faucets may come from a distant mountain valley or a well in the backyard, but regardless of its source, your water may contain some surprises that you would not want to drink. Even if it looks clear and tastes good, drinking water can carry a variety of chemical and biological passengers that might make you and your family sick, or even threaten your life.

This chapter describes the contaminants—from asbestos to zinc—commonly found in drinking water in the United States, where those contaminants come from, and the health effects and other problems they can cause.

## WHAT'S IN THE WATER BESIDES WATER?

Drinking water contaminants can be divided into five categories, summarized in Table 1. Each of the categories, and examples of the contaminants in those categories, are described in detail in the remainder of this chapter.

These drinking water pollutants come from a variety of sources, ranging from human sewage and industrial waste to pesticide runoff and backyard dumping.

Not all contaminants come from human sources; even a pristine mountain watershed can contain pathogens carried by livestock or wild animals, and some toxic minerals leach

**TABLE I**

## Five Categories of Drinking Water Contaminants

| PATHOGENS | INORGANIC CHEMICALS AND METALS | SYNTHETIC ORGANIC CHEMICALS | RADIOACTIVE SUBSTANCES | ADDITIVES |
|---|---|---|---|---|
| Bacteria | Lead | Pesticides | Radium | Chlorine |
| Viruses | Nitrates | PCBs | Radon | Fluoride |
| Protozoa | Arsenic | Dioxins | Reactor Wastes | Coagulents |

from naturally occurring mineral layers in the ground. But most of the materials described in this chapter get into our drinking water as the result of some human activity.

## PATHOGENS

Pathogens are microorganisms, living creatures so small you need a microscope to see them. They include bacteria, viruses, and protozoa; enter drinking water from human sewage or animal feces; and cause diseases ranging from dysentery and hepatitis to giardiasis and Legionnaire's disease.

Pathogens in drinking water sicken an estimated 940,000 people a year and kill several hundred, usually those with poor resistance to disease, including the very old, the very young, AIDS sufferers, and others weakened by serious illness, a recent organ transplant, or cancer therapy. Pathogens also cause higher miscarriage rates among pregnant women. In the past decade, more than 100 waterborne disease outbreaks were reported in U.S. drinking water systems, although according to the Environmental Protection Agency, the actual number of cases may be several hundred times higher because the majority of cases go unreported.

Waterborne diseases often attack the human gastrointestinal system, and, although their symptoms can be severe and debilitating, today they are rarely as fatal as they were at the turn of the century when cholera and typhoid were widespread. Outbreaks usually cause acute symptoms that in otherwise healthy people will go away once the immune system kicks in or the disease is treated, as opposed to cases of chemical contamination, which cause chronic, or lasting, health effects. Due to the incubation period of the infecting microorganisms, the symptoms of infection by a waterborne disease often appear days or even weeks after a person has drunk contaminated water.

## Sources of Pathogen Contamination

Pathogen contamination of both groundwater and surface water supplies most often results from inadequate control over pathogen sources such as animal feedlot runoff and sewage overflow. While groundwater has a greater degree of inherent insulation from naturally occurring microorganisms such as *Giardia lamblia*, pathogens associated with human activity, ranging from feedlot runoff to sewage and septic-tank overflows, can equally threaten both groundwater and surface water systems.

*Groundwater systems.* Small drinking water systems and individual wells utilizing groundwater often have a high risk of pathogen contamination; these systems often rely on untreated groundwater. During one ten-year period studied, more than half of all reported outbreaks of waterborne disease were attributed to contaminated groundwater that was either not treated or not treated adequately.

Groundwater pathogen contamination most often results from septic-tank or cesspool overflow or drainage. Contamination can occur, for example, in areas where septic tanks or cesspools overlay a water table that rises and falls seasonally, or in areas of uneven geology. Improper well construction and poorly cased wells can allow contaminated groundwater and surface water to enter the well. Domestic animal feedlots also release pathogens into the groundwater and surface water, and are a major source of contamination of drinking water wells.

*Surface water systems.* Runoff from farms, feedlots, and other areas where there is intensive animal husbandry is a major source of surface water contamination. In addition, many large water systems have combined sewage outflows that allow raw or partially treated sewage to mix with storm runoff and drain directly into open waterways during heavy rains. Due to overburdened treatment plants, outdated technology, or, in some instances, failure by water systems and government agencies to protect watersheds, systems fail to filter and adequately disinfect their water to substantially reduce disease-carrying organisms. This is the leading cause of pathogen contamination of drinking water from surface water supplies. Strong source water protection programs for watersheds can substantially reduce or virtually eliminate dangerous levels of bacteria and other pathogens in source water.

In 1993, outbreaks of *E. coli* bacteria in the water supply forced Washington, D.C., and New York City to alert residents in affected neighborhoods not to drink their tap water. The Washington, D.C., outbreak was tied to an improperly operating treatment plant, and the New York City outbreak was attributed to inadequate protection of the city's reservoirs from contamination, in this case by bird droppings.

### Bacteria

Bacteria are single-celled organisms that flourish in a variety of environments ranging from the volcanic vents in the bottom of the sea to the snowfields of the highest mountains. Bacterial pathogens found in drinking water cause symptoms ranging from mild diarrhea to serious diseases including bacillary dysentery, cholera, typhoid fever, and Legionnaire's disease.

The advent of chlorination in the early 1900s put a major dent in the impact of bacterial contamination of drinking water, nearly eliminating cholera and typhoid in this country. Even so, poorly treated or untreated drinking water may still carry bacterial pathogens that can cause serious illness. In

1993, the presence of high total coliforms and *E. coli* in the drinking water of New York City and Washington, D.C., forced residents in affected neighborhoods to drink bottled water until proper treatment methods could be applied to the municipal water supply. Chlorination and filtration at a central water treatment plant can effectively eliminate most harmful bacteria from drinking water supplies.

*Legionella.* Legionnaire's disease, which killed 34 people in Philadelphia in 1976 and caused the evacuation of the cruise liner *Horizon* in 1994, is caused by *Legionella pneumophila* bacteria. Up to 100,000 people per year may become ill with Legionnaire's disease although, like most waterborne diseases in the United States, it is rarely fatal. Even so, the bacteria were fatal to six of forty-five victims in Massachusetts, Rhode Island, and Michigan in 1993. *Legionella* bacteria have been found in the shower heads, faucets, and hot water tanks of hospitals, hotels, factories, and homes. The 1993 outbreaks were all attributed to bacteria buildups in cooling towers. In fact, presence of the bacteria is generally associated with stagnant water in human-made systems such as storage tanks, cooling towers, and plumbing components and fixtures. No outbreak has ever been directly associated with a natural waterway such as a lake, stream, or pond.

### Protozoa: *Giardia* and *Cryptosporidium*

Parasitic protozoa such as *Giardia lamblia* and *Cryptosporidium* are common in the lakes, rivers, and streams that provide many communities with drinking water. Although during their life cycles *Giardia* and *Cryptosporidium* permutate through various physical stages, it is during their stage as cysts that they are the biggest threat to human health and the most difficult to kill. Published reports by leading researchers on *Crypto* have estimated that from 86 to 95 percent of surface water systems tested have *Crypto* in their supply water, and that more than 50 percent have *Crypto* in their treated, finished water. *Giardia*, a microorganism that causes painful intestinal sickness, may exist in low concentrations even in remote, undisturbed watersheds. It is most common in the Rocky Mountain states, the Pacific Northwest, and New England. Almost half of all waterborne outbreaks in community water systems are due to *Giardia*, making it the most commonly identified pathogen. Although protozoan cysts are highly resistant to disinfection by chlorination, the combination of optimized, modern filtration and chlorination is considered highly effective in reducing *Giardia* in water supplies.

### Viruses

Viruses are organisms so small they can only be seen with a scanning electron microscope, which makes them very difficult to monitor and detect in drinking water. Viruses that infest drinking water include Hepatitis A and the Norwalk virus, which is reported to cause more than 20 percent of all outbreaks of waterborne disease in the United States. Many of the unidentifiable causes of waterborne disease may be attributable to viruses.

Most water treatment plants were not designed to remove viruses, and treatment designed to reduce bacteria does not necessarily eliminate viruses as well. Even so, the Environmental Protection Agency claims that conventional treatment plants using optimized filtration and disinfection methods can achieve 99.99 percent effectiveness in eliminating the viruses that cause human illness.

## Preventing Pathogens

Sewage overflows, barnyard waste, and animal fecal material from feedlots, stockyards, pastures, and grazing land all contribute to the presence of parasitic pathogens and other harmful microorganisms in drinking water.

The best treatment for these microscopic pests is keeping them out of the water to begin with. This means improving sewage treatment facilities that currently allow overflow into rivers and lakes, strengthening farm and ranch management practices, and increasing watershed protection on grazing and range land.

Water treatment methods effective at virtually eliminating pathogens date from the early 1900s, when chlorination, filtration, and sedimentation systems were first installed by many water utilities. Chlorine alone will kill many waterborne pathogens, but filtration is required to ensure effective reduction of viruses and parasitic protozoa such as *Giardia*. Additionally, filtration prior to chlorination can reduce the formation of carcinogenic chlorination by-products that form when chlorine reacts with naturally occurring, otherwise harmless organic matter that enters the water from natural sources. Unfortunately, less than 20 percent of surface water–supplied utilities have watershed protection programs that meet the EPA's minimal standards for avoiding filtration, and more than eighty big surface water systems, which provide water to 4 million people, have neither installed filtration nor protected their watersheds, in violation of EPA rules.

## INORGANIC CHEMICALS AND METALS

A variety of toxic chemicals, minerals, and metals can contaminate drinking water supplies either as the result of natural processes of the environment or, more commonly, as the result of human activity.

Among the metals and inorganic chemical contaminants that threaten drinking water supplies, lead, arsenic, mercury, and cadmium are probably the most important.

### Sources of Lead in Drinking Water

Among the contaminants of special concern is lead, which is commonly used in pipes, faucets, and the solder used to join components of plumbing systems in homes and other buildings. In fact, the word "plumbing" derives from the Latin

## Questions About Turbidity

### What is turbidity?

Turbidity is the cloudy appearance caused by small particles suspended in water. These particles may consist of naturally occurring algae, clay, microorganisms, silt, organic chemicals, or decaying vegetation, or they may consist of chemical wastes.

### Is turbidity bad?

Yes. Turbidity can interfere with the disinfection process, and may absorb or bond with toxic substances, preventing their removal during treatment. Also, some normally harmless organic materials that cause turbidity, such as decaying plant matter, can form cancer-causing compounds when exposed to chlorine during water treatment. For these reasons, it is important to reduce turbidity to make water safe to drink.

### What can I do about turbidity?

Reducing runoff in a system's watershed is often highly effective. In addition, properly operating water treatment plants should reduce turbidity to acceptable levels. Chapter 3 describes how you can find out about the quality of your drinking water, and Chapters 5 and 6 offer suggestions for what to do if your water has high turbidity or other types of contaminants.

word for lead, *plumbum*. The corrosive action of water leaches lead from pipes, well pumps, and faucets. People drinking or cooking with lead-tainted water show elevated lead levels in their blood and risk severe, negative, long-term health effects. According to the EPA, more than 800 cities in the United States have water that exceeds the EPA's "action level" for lead and require better treatment to reduce lead hazards.

Even low levels of lead intake can cause fetal damage and delayed neurological and physical development in children, and high blood pressure, heart attacks, kidney damage, reproductive dysfunction, and strokes in adults. At higher levels of intake, lead is classified as a probable carcinogen as well.

Over half of U.S. cities still use lead or lead-lined pipes or plumbing components, which are the primary source of lead in drinking water. Lead also enters surface water from atmospheric particulates created by leaded gasoline combustion, ore smelting, and the burning of fossil fuels. In groundwater, lead leaches from soil and rock minerals that the water flows through.

## Reducing Lead in Drinking Water

If you have pipes, solder, or faucets made of lead or lead alloys, the most important factors determining the amount of the lead that leaches into your water are the water's corrosiveness and the time of contact between the water and the lead-containing components.

The first water out of the faucet and pipes in the morning will have the highest lead levels because it has been sitting in lead-containing faucets and pipes all night, so if you suspect or know you have lead in your water, the first precaution to take is to flush your lines by running water in the sink for a few minutes if it has been unused for several hours, at least until the water cools, indicating that it is coming from pipes outside the house. Use the flushed water to water plants or for other household uses, rather than waste it. Water softeners also increase corrosiveness, so if you know you have a lead problem, don't soften your water.

In some relatively unusual cases, lead has been used in service lines running from the water main into people's homes. In these cases, flushing the water may actually result in *increased* lead exposure. The only way to know for sure is to test for lead in the first water out of your faucet in the morning, and test again after flushing the line for a few minutes.

## Metal Solvency and Corrosiveness

The amount of lead and other metals in plumbing materials that will dissolve into water is determined by the water's corrosivity, a combination of its acidity (pH), alkalinity, and softness. Lower pH and alkalinity mean more corrosive water; so does softness. Softening your water increases the chances that it will leach lead and other metals from the pipes and fixtures that bring it to your glass. About 80 percent of public water systems have moderately to highly corrosive water.

### Sources of Arsenic in Drinking Water

Arsenic, a well-known poison in strong doses, is a potent carcinogen even at very low levels of intake. Three hundred thousand people may drink water containing over 50 parts per billion (ppb) of arsenic, the EPA maximum allowable level and an amount that may pose a 1-in-50 cancer risk. Worse yet, 2.5 *million* people may be drinking water with over 25 ppb, and 35 million people may be drinking water with more than 2 ppb, enough to create a 1-in-1,000 cancer risk, about the same as from second-hand smoke. Studies have also indicated that arsenic intake can lead to abnormal fetal development, blood disorders, cardiovascular disease, central nervous system disorders, and diabetes mellitus.

Arsenic is found associated with the ores of copper, lead, zinc, iron, manganese, and uranium. It is released in smelting and is leached from mine tailings. Some pesticides used on cotton and tobacco contain arsenic, as do certain wood preservatives, sheep dips, and livestock feed supplements. Burning of anthracite coal, the kind of coal mined in the eastern United States, releases arsenic to the atmosphere.

### Sources of Mercury in Drinking Water

Mercury is most toxic in its organic form, methyl mercury, but most industrial discharge of the metal is in its metallic form.

## Bioaccumulation

Mercury, like lead, bioaccumulates, which means its levels increase as it moves up the food chain. For example, concentrations of mercury in fish can be many times higher than in contaminated water. Tuna and swordfish are primary accumulators, but mercury will build up in most animals, including humans. Diet is a greater source of human exposure to mercury than drinking water, although mercury gets into the food chain first through the water. As with all heavy metal contaminants, pollution prevention is the most effective long-term approach to reducing exposure to mercury.

Even so, bacteria in underwater sediments can transform mercury to its organic form. The primary health effects of mercury intake are damage to the central nervous system (and associated neurological diseases) and brain damage.

Batteries, electrical switching equipment, and measuring and monitoring instruments often use mercury components. Mercury is also used as a preservative in paint, fabric, cosmetics, and pharmaceuticals; as a wood preservative; and in the manufacture of plastics and organic chemicals. Mercury is released to the environment during the manufacture and disposal of these products; from oil- and coal-burning energy plants; and from metal smelters.

### Sources of Cadmium in Drinking Water

Cadmium is classified in the same category as lead and arsenic in its potential as a health hazard. It is found in naturally occurring minerals, but generally only enters water sources during mining, extraction, manufacture, and disposal.

Cadmium is used for electroplating, in paint and pigments, in PVC and plastics manufacturing, in nickel-cadmium battery production, and in the manufacture of alloys and solder. Leaching from batteries in landfills and from industrial and mining waste contributes to cadmium in drinking water, as do emissions from smelters.

Intake of cadmium is associated with hypertension, lung damage, impairment of the cardiovascular and central nervous systems, and liver and kidney damage. Cadmium is also believed to cause genetic damage and to affect fetal development negatively. The kidney is believed to be the main target of cadmium in the body.

## Other Metals

*Antimony.* Antimony is a semimetallic element used in alloys with other metals and in compounds in paints, ceramics, electronics, fire retardants, solder, and storage batteries. Ingestion of antimony has been linked to cancer.

*Barium.* Barium is a metal used in paint pigments, rat poisons, epoxy sealants, water softeners, and fireworks. It leaches into water from natural deposits, waste dumps, and industrial pollution. Barium intake is associated with liver dysfunctions.

*Beryllium.* Beryllium is a silver-gray metal known for its light weight and strength. It is used in x-ray tubes and nuclear reactors, as well as in aerospace and defense manufacturing. Beryllium toxicity causes bone and lung damage.

*Chromium.* Chromium is widely used in a range of industrial products and processes, and because it is highly water soluble, chromium compounds often wind up in rivers and streams.

Chromium is used in the manufacture of chrome alloys and platings, paints and pigments, photographics, textiles, ceramics, glass, explosives, batteries, rubber tires, and paper. Like other metals, chromium is leached into water supplies from mining wastes.

Health effects linked to chromium intake include liver and kidney damage, internal bleeding, respiratory disorders, and genetic damage. Chromium has also been associated with digestive tract cancers.

*Copper.* Copper contamination of water is generally of concern due to its ability to stain sinks, tubs, and fixtures, although health effects have been associated only with excessive ingestion. Copper at trace levels is considered an essential nutrient, necessary for many enzyme reactions within the body. Some evidence links elevated levels of copper with digestive disorders, liver and kidney damage, and, in cases of acute poisoning, anemia.

Copper is released by the iron and steel industries; in mining, smelting and refining, and coal burning; in the production of copper wire and fungicides; and in the manufacture of plumbing fittings and fixtures, which are the primary source of copper in drinking water, especially fittings and fixtures made of copper and brass.

*Nickel.* Nickel is a metal used in batteries, in chemical manufacture, and in the production of stainless steel. Nickel intake is associated with heart and liver damage.

*Thallium.* Thallium is a soft metal with a lustrous, silver-gray appearance. It is used in insecticides, pharmaceuticals, metal alloys, and glass. Over time, thallium ingestion leads to kidney and liver damage as well as brain and intestinal disorders.

## Non-Metallic Inorganics

### Asbestos

A well-documented carcinogen, asbestos is present in the water wherever asbestos-cement (AC) is used in water mains, which is almost everywhere in the country. Low levels of intake have been associated with kidney, bone, and blood disease and disorders of the nervous system. Repair of AC pipes releases asbestos into the water, where it often passes undetected into the drinking supply.

### Cyanide

Cyanide is widely used in insecticides, in making pigments, in metal refining, and in the manufacture of plastics. Cyanide is also used to leach precious metals from their ores in cyanide-heap leach mines in the western United States. In small quantities, most cyanide compounds are lethal poisons that cause respiratory failure and death. Long-term effects of low-level cyanide exposure include thyroid damage and nervous system degeneration.

### Nitrates and Nitrites

Nitrogen-containing compounds, nitrates and nitrites are released from agricultural runoff, yard fertilizers, septic tanks and sewers, and certain industrial processes utilizing ammonia. Nitrate ingestion can cause intestinal problems in adults and oxygen deprivation in babies, called the blue-baby syndrome. A recent nationwide study by the EPA detected elevated levels of nitrates in 52 percent of domestic water wells. Nitrates also contribute to the formation of nitrites and nitrosamines, which are carcinogens.

### Selenium

Selenium is used in a variety of industrial processes, including glassmaking, cosmetics, photoelectronics, and rubber manufacture, and in pesticides for agricultural crops. Selenium from natural deposits in the ground has leached into irrigation projects in several western states and has poisoned migratory waterfowl in open reservoirs, ponds, and lakes.

A vital human nutrient in minuscule quantities, selenium is toxic in higher concentrations, leading to liver damage and other illnesses.

## Nuisance Minerals

Water softening systems improve the cleaning effectiveness of soap and detergent, although they remove calcium and magnesium, which cause hardness in water but are also considered essential human nutrients. Removing these minerals also increases corrosivity, leading to lead problems.

Iron and manganese are two metals that stain laundry and washroom fixtures, but are not considered health risks.

# SYNTHETIC ORGANIC CHEMICALS (SOCS)

Organic chemicals are chemicals that contain carbon. Some organic chemicals, like those released by decaying vegetation, occur naturally and by themselves tend not to pose health problems when they get in our drinking water. Synthetic organic chemicals (SOCs), on the other hand, are all human-made and, because they do not occur naturally in the environment, are often toxic to living organisms, including humans.

## *Sources of SOCs*

Modern industry uses synthetic organic chemicals in everything from pesticides to plastic baby carriages. SOCs include PCBs, 2,4-D (a common home pesticide), carbon tetrachloride, aldicarb, chlordane, dioxin, xylene, phenols, and thousands of other synthetic chemicals. Although more than 50,000 SOCs are in commercial production, little or no toxicity data exists for 64 percent of the pesticides, 74 percent of the cosmetic ingredients, and 79 percent of all the synthetic chemicals in use in the United States. It is therefore difficult to determine the safety of many substances found in the water supply. Even so, the health risks of a wide range of synthetic chemicals are known.

One important class of SOCs is pesticides. Pesticides are chemicals designed to kill living organisms and to be spread on the land. The fact that they damage ecosystems, endanger wildlife, and threaten human health should therefore come as no surprise. Yet while evidence of the widespread environmental and human health risks from pesticide use continues to grow, the sales and use of pesticides continue to climb, as do industry claims for the benefits of continued pesticide application.

A 1995 study of twenty-nine midwestern cities and towns by the Washington, D.C.–based nonprofit Environmental Working Group found pesticide residues in the drinking water of

## SOCs Currently Regulated Under the Safe Drinking Water Act

Acrylamide
Alachlor
Adipate,(di(2-ethylhexyl))
Aldicarb
Aldicarbsulfone
Aldicarbsulfoxide
Atrazine
Benzene
Carbofuran
Carbon tetrachloride
Chlordane
Chlorobenzene
Dalapon
Dichloromethane
2,4,-D
o-Dichlorobenzene
p-Dichlorobenzene
1,2-Dichloroethane
1,1-Dichloroethane
cis-1,2-Dichloroethylene
trans-1,2-Dichloroethylene

Dibromochloropropane
1,2-Dichloropropane
Dinoseb
Dioxin
Diquat
Endothall
Epichlorohydrin
Ethylbenzene
Ethylenedibromide
Glyphosate
Heptachlor
Heptachlorepoxide
Hexachlorobenzene
Hexachlorocyclopentadiene
Oxamyl (Vydate)
PAHs (benzo (a) pyrene)
Phthalate,(di(2-ethylhexyl))
Picloram
Simazine
1,2,4-Trichlorobenzene
Trichloroethylene
Trihalomethanes (THMs)
1,1,1-Trichloroethylene
1,1,2-Trichloroethane
Vinyl chloride

nearly all of them. In Danville, Illinois, the level of the Du-Pont-made weed killer cyanazine was thirty-four times the federal standard. In Fort Wayne, Indiana, one glass of tap water contained nine kinds of pesticides. These pesticide levels often do not violate EPA standards because the regulations are based on annual averages, but intense spraying during the spring planting season boosts concentrations in drinking water to extremely high levels during subsequent months.

## Pesticides in America

- Each year, approximately 2.6 billion pounds of pesticides are used in the United States.

- According to the EPA, at least sixty-six of the 300 pesticides used on food are potentially carcinogenic.

- Since 1945, pesticide use in the United States has increased tenfold, and at the same time crop loss from insects has increased almost twofold, from about 7 percent to 13 percent.

- With increased aircraft application, most pesticides are poorly targeted—less than 2/10 of a percent of the chemicals applied ever reach their intended target.

- The average child receives four times more exposure than an adult to eight widely used carcinogenic pesticides in food.

- DDT has been found in animals in the Antarctic and other areas where the pesticide was never sprayed.

- The incidence of several types of cancer thought to be associated with chemical exposure has risen since World War II, a time period during which the use of synthetic pesticides has become increasingly widespread. Studies of cancer mortalities indicate an increased risk for users of certain farm pesticides, and for those who live in proximity to chemical companies, petrochemical plants, and oil refineries.

This was the first study of its kind and revealed "widespread contamination of tap water with many different pesticides at levels that present serious health risks."

About 50 percent of urban and suburban pesticide use is categorized as non-agricultural. These applications include preservation of building materials; treatment of food containers; spraying of school yards, roadsides, golf courses, parks, and utility right-of-ways; and home use in backyards and gardens. Almost all modern pesticides are synthetic organic chemicals, many of which pose serious threats to human health when found in drinking water.

Another important source of groundwater contamination

by SOCs is leakage from underground storage tanks, which hold everything from gasoline to chemical and nuclear waste. According to recent estimates, up to one-fourth of the 3 to 10 million underground storage tanks in the United States are likely to be leaking.

Of the 129 contaminants listed by the EPA as priority pollutants, 114 are SOCs. Many pesticides and other SOCs are not included in the priority pollutant list; therefore their industrial discharge into the land, air, and water is not monitored.

## Health Effects of SOCs

Health effects of exposure to SOCs vary widely, depending on the specific chemical. Documented effects include organ and skin disease, blood disorders, neurological damage, genetic and reproductive effects, and cancer. In fact, SOCs include the most toxic and persistent poisons produced by modern chemical technology.

In addition to intake from drinking and cooking water contaminated by SOCs, skin absorption and absorption by inhalation increase exposure. The greatest concern with respect to inhalation is hot showers, where volatile SOCs easily evaporate in a confined area and high levels can be inhaled.

## RADIOACTIVE MATERIALS

According to the Environmental Protection Agency, some 50 million Americans face increased cancer risk due to radioactive contamination of their drinking water. Radionuclides, the radioactive metals and minerals that cause this contamination, come from natural and human-made sources.

## Naturally Occurring Radionuclides

Naturally occurring radioactive minerals move from underground rockbeds and geologic formations into the underground streams flowing through them, primarily affecting groundwater. Due to their occurrence in drinking water and their effects on human health, the natural radionuclides of most concern are radium-226, radium-228, radon-222, and uranium.

High levels of natural radionuclides are generally associated with certain regions of the country; the geology of an area is the major factor in determining the likelihood of finding natural radioactive elements in drinking water. If you live in a region with granite substrata or known radioactive minerals, you may have radioactivity in your drinking water.

### Uranium

Uranium has been found in surface water and groundwater, but concentrations in groundwater are usually higher. Uranium in groundwater is most often found in the Plains states, the Rockies, and the Great Basin. Parts of California have a high potential for elevated uranium levels in water because of the presence of granite rocks, and isolated cases of high uranium levels in water have been found in New England as well.

### Radium

Radium in water is found primarily in groundwater, and occurs most often in the states bordering the Gulf of Mexico and areas of Minnesota, Wisconsin, Iowa, Illinois, and Missouri.

### Radon

Radon is a colorless, odorless gas created by the natural decay of minerals in the soil. It enters homes through cracks in the foundation, through crawl spaces and unfinished basements, and in tainted water and is considered the second leading cause of lung cancer in the United States, following cigarette smoking. Information on how you can test the air and water in your home for radon is provided in Chapter 5.

## Human-Made Radionuclides

Some 200 human-made radioactive elements and compounds are believed to be potential drinking water contaminants. All are products of the nuclear industry and all are carcinogenic. Common human-made radionuclides include cesium-137 and strontium-90. Millions of pounds of uranium have been released from nuclear power plants and processing plants into the air, ground, and water.

Radioactivity from human activity enters water supplies from nuclear power plant leaks and discharges, nuclear materials processing facilities, weapons testing, medical waste disposal, waste depository leakage, and nuclear accidents. Even mining for non-radioactive metals and minerals can expose buried radioactive minerals to wind erosion and leaching by rainfall and runoff. If the river, reservoir, or mountain runoff feeding your water supply is downstream from any mining area or nuclear facility, you should have your water tested for radioactivity.

## ADDITIVES

Certain chemicals are added deliberately to the drinking water supply for a variety of reasons. They include chlorine, fluoride, and flocculents. Among them, chlorine and its by-products are of greatest concern.

## Chlorine and Disinfection By-Products

The practice of adding chlorine to drinking water to neutralize bacteria and other waterborne disease–causing organisms has been used in the United States since 1908, and chlorine has proven to be an effective disinfectant for drinking water. Chlorine is added to water at treatment facilities as free chlorine, chlorine dioxide, or chloramine. In 1974, it was discovered that chlorine reacts with naturally occurring organic chemicals that are left in the water by contact with soil and decaying vegetation, and forms a group of chemicals called disinfection by-products (DBPs). Among these DBPs, chemicals called trihalomethanes (THMs) have received the most attention. THMs include chloroform and three other chemicals. About 200 additional DBPs, called chlorinated organics, form in a manner similar to THMs, but many of them have only been identified tentatively. Other DBPs include halo-acetic acids, chlorite, and bromate.

DBPs are most common in surface water drinking supplies. About 90 percent of small municipal water systems use groundwater that generally does not contain decaying vegetation, is therefore low in natural organics, and so is not generally chlorinated.

## Health Effects of Disinfection By-Products

Well-documented studies published in leading medical journals have concluded that disinfection by-products are associated with 10,000 or more rectal and bladder cancers each year in the United States, and have linked the chemicals to pancreatic cancer as well. Additional studies by the U.S. Public Health Service and the New Jersey Department of Health indicate that these chemicals may also cause major birth defects, including neurological disorders and spinal defects. The dilemma presented by these findings is that without chlorination, dangerous pathogens may proliferate in drinking supplies, but with chlorine, lethal DBPs may be formed. The solution to the dilemma is to protect watersheds, in order to substantially reduce organic loading, and to remove the organic materials prior to chlorination, by use of granular activated carbon filtration or other means. Ultimately, a switch to non-chlorine primary disinfectants, such as ozone, is also a very promising approach widely used in Europe and some U.S. cities. But many experts believe that currently there is still no alternative to using low levels of chlorine in the distribution system as a "residual disinfectant" to keep microbes from regrowing or re-entering the system. But these low levels of chlorine, combined with reduced levels of organic matter in the water, yield low levels of disinfection by-products.

## Fluoride

Although the medical and dental communities have generally embraced water fluoridation as a means of fighting tooth decay, some studies refute its effectiveness in preventing tooth decay and some indicate that it is carcinogenic. Other studies have found fluoridation to weaken the immune system and interfere with the body's enzyme operation. Most Western developed nations don't fluoridate their water. Although a detailed discussion of the issue is beyond the scope of this book, Colin Ingram, the author of four books and studies on drinking water–related issues, has concluded that

> [w]ater fluoridation is one of the most irrational and health-threatening programs ever offered to the American public. I firmly believe the harm from fluoridated drinking water far outweighs the benefit, and I recommend that you and your children do not drink fluoridated water.
>
> (Colin Ingram, *The Drinking Water Book*, Berkeley, CA, Ten Speed Press, 1991, p. 25)

Even so, there remains a huge debate among reasonable public health officials on this question, and whether the risks of fluoridation outweigh its benefits seems a question still to be answered.

## Flocculents

Flocculents are chemicals added to water to make particles clump together, to improve the effectiveness of filtration. Some of the most common flocculents are polyelectrolytes, chemicals with constituents that cause cancer and birth defects and are banned for use by several other countries. Although the EPA classifies them as "probable human carcinogens," it still allows their use to continue. Acrylamide and epichlorohydrin are two flocculents used in the United States that are known to be associated with probable cancer risk.

**2**

⬡

# The Broken Promise of Pure Water

**W**ouldn't it be nice to know that the water coming out of your faucets was pure and healthy to drink, free from the chemical and biological contaminants described in Chapter 1? You might think that here in the United States, with our modern technology and scientific knowledge, clean, safe drinking water would be guaranteed in public water systems. As a matter of fact, the federal government set out to accomplish that very objective in the early 1970s. Unfortunately, more than twenty years later, safe drinking water remains a promise yet to be fulfilled.

This chapter describes ongoing efforts by the government to guarantee the public clean drinking water, the major obstacles to those efforts, and the opportunities available for citizens to help overcome those obstacles.

## THE SAFE DRINKING WATER ACT

To ensure that the drinking water supply of the United States would be safe and healthy, Congress passed the Safe Drinking Water Act (SDWA) in 1974 and strengthened it in 1986. The SDWA requires the Environmental Protection Agency (EPA), an agency of the federal government under the direction of the president, to undertake the following measures:

- Identify drinking water contaminants that could pose a health risk to the American public

- Define maximum allowable levels or treatment techniques for those contaminants

- Establish and carry out enforcement procedures to ensure compliance with those maximum levels

The EPA is required by the Safe Drinking Water Act to regulate all public water systems, defined in the SDWA as all systems that provide drinking water to fifteen or more homes or at least twenty-five individuals. These public water systems are then divided by the EPA into community and non-community systems, as indicated in Table 2.

**TABLE 2**

## Two Types of Public Drinking Water Systems

|  | COMMUNITY SYSTEMS | NON-COMMUNITY SYSTEMS |
|---|---|---|
| Definition | Serve year-round residents such as homeowners and apartment dwellers | Hotels, schools, hospitals, and other systems whose customers are not year-round |
| Number of Systems in United States | More than 58,000 | More than 140,000 |
| Number of People Served | 245 million | 22 million |
| Applicable Standards | All EPA standards apply | Only coliform, turbidity, and nitrate standards apply |

## Maximum Contaminant Levels

The Safe Drinking Water Act requires all community systems, which together provide drinking water to almost 250 million people, to meet a set of contaminant standards established by the EPA. These standards are called the Primary Drinking Water Standards. For each contaminant listed by the EPA in the Primary Drinking Water Standards, a maximum contaminant level (MCL) is set, which is typically measured in parts per million (ppm) or milligrams per liter (mpl), equivalent measures. The EPA Primary Drinking Water Standards as of 1994 are listed in Appendix A at the back of this book.

## Secondary Standards

Secondary Drinking Water Standards are unenforceable federal guidelines regarding the taste, odor, and color, as well as certain other non-aesthetic effects, of drinking water. The EPA recommends these standards to the states as reasonable goals, but federal law does not directly require water systems to comply with them. States are to adopt their own regulations governing these concerns.

## Treatment Techniques

For some contaminants, such as lead and copper, rather than a parts-per-million limit, the EPA sets a treatment technique standard (TT), which requires specific treatment measures if contaminants exceed established "action levels." The surface water treatment rule requires surface water systems to prove that they have low levels of *Giardia*, bacteria, viruses, and turbidity; and they must either protect their watersheds or install mandatory filtration equipment.

## Monitoring, Reporting, and Notification Rules

In addition to setting maximum levels for identified contaminants, the EPA established rules that require water systems to periodically test their water for contaminants and report the results to state or federal agencies. Without regular and accurate testing and reporting, the EPA and state agencies cannot determine whether systems are keeping contaminant levels below the maximum levels established in the regulations. Unfortunately, monitoring and testing by water systems has fallen far behind the requirements of the Safe Drinking Water Act. In one two-year period, more than 217,500 reporting violations were recorded by the EPA from systems providing water to 100 million Americans. The severity of the problem can hardly be overstated.

The Safe Drinking Water Act requires public water systems to notify their customers when contaminant levels violate EPA standards. The notification requirements vary depending on the severity of the violation and can range from a notice in your water bill or in the newspaper to an alert on all local television and radio stations. However, in most cases, according to the Government Accounting Office, the public is *not* informed of known violations of health standards.

## States Retain Enforcement Responsibility

States have the option of taking primary responsibility for enforcement of systems within their borders, and all fifty states have chosen to accept this task rather than have the EPA tell them what steps they must take to meet the federal standards. In cases where states fail to enforce EPA standards, the EPA is supposed to step in and take enforcement action on its own.

## Widespread Violations and Lax Enforcement

By 1994, the EPA had set maximum contaminant level standards (MCLs) for eighty-four substances and pathogens, and had instituted enforcement mechanisms to promote compliance. The EPA had also established a time frame for MCLs for additional contaminants and created a list of pollutants to be considered as future additions to the MCLs roster.

Unfortunately, the failures of the Safe Drinking Water Act have been numerous. For one thing, many dangerous pollutants are not listed or will not be regulated for several years to come. These contaminants include dozens of synthetic organic chemicals, some of which are suspected carcinogens; certain radioactive materials; *Cryptosporidium* and other pathogen contaminants; and even disinfection by-products created by chlorination or other disinfection techniques. For some listed contaminants, allowable levels are far too high, higher than those allowed by other developed countries. For example, under the Safe Drinking Water Act, the EPA has proposed an MCL for total trihalomethanes (THMs) of 100 parts per billion. A study conducted by the National Academy of Sciences, however, concluded in 1987 that 100 parts per billion is not a stringent enough standard for THMs. In fact, a report published in the *American Journal of Public Health*, based on a series of more than ten studies, concluded that 10,000 people get rectal or bladder cancer each year from exposure to trihalomethanes and other by-products of chlorine disinfection.

The record of enforcement under the Safe Drinking Water Act has been exceedingly poor as well. According to a 1995 report published by the Natural Resources Defense Council (NRDC), a New York–based environmental organization, in 1993 and 1994, 53 million Americans drank water from systems that were either more contaminated than EPA health standards allow or did not treat their water as required to protect consumers against lead, parasites, and bacteria. During the two-year period covered in the study, the NRDC found that more than 25,000 public water systems violated EPA rules a total of 180,726 times. *Of those violations, fewer than 3,500 received any formal enforcement actions, virtually all with little or no penalties.*

Surprisingly, instead of responding to this drinking water crisis by strengthening the law and stepping up enforcement, in 1994 Congress turned in the opposite direction and tried to *weaken* the Safe Drinking Water Act. Why this happened, and what we can do to get our elected officials to improve the reliability and quality of our drinking water, will be discussed in Chapter 7.

## CLEAN WATER: POSSIBILITIES AND REALITIES

Despite the widespread failure of the Environmental Protection Agency and the states to provide reliably clean drinking water to the American public, that possibility remains a realistic goal. The challenge is to replace inadequate treatment facilities with better ones, or to modernize aging plants that can no longer do their job.

### How Water Treatment Centers Are Supposed to Work

Public water treatment efforts began in the mid-1800s with the recognition that waterborne bacteria carried diseases; most notably cholera. In the early 1900s, U.S. cities began to use techniques including coagulation, filtration, and disinfection to remove dangerous organisms and materials from drinking water. Coagulants such as alum cause particles in the water to clump together, so that filters can more easily remove them. Sedimentation ponds let particles drop out of the water as it sits motionless in large pools. Sand or charcoal filtration traps contaminants as water seeps through layers of sand or pulverized coal.

The use of these early treatment methods significantly improved drinking water quality in the United States and Europe in the early 1900s. But population pressure, the advent of widespread mining and logging in watersheds, and the growing production and use of modern chemicals have rendered these early water treatment methods inadequate and have left the public exposed to an onslaught of dangerous contaminants.

### The Basics of Providing Clean Water

The best way to assure a safe public water supply is with a three-tiered line of defense, beginning with protecting the source of the water supply and then adding basic and advanced purification methods.

## Protect the Source

Surprisingly, few public water systems make aggressive efforts to stop contaminants from entering their watersheds or groundwater supplies to begin with. In fact, a 1994 study found that less than 20 percent of surface water–supplied systems have significant watershed protection measures in place, and less than 22 percent of groundwater systems have implemented measures to protect their well fields from major sources of pollution. Even so, protecting the source is almost always technically easier and less expensive than removing contaminants once they enter the water. Some very large municipal systems, including portions of New York City's, have made watershed protection their first line of defense and thus far have averted the need for advanced purification. As the pressures of development near these watersheds continue to mount, the value of stringent watershed protection will increase as well.

## Basic Purification Methods

There are five basic water purification methods for public water supplies; sedimentation, aeration, filtration, disinfection, and coagulation. Most of these techniques are at least 100 years old, and some are much older than that. These techniques are summarized in Table 3.

Ninety percent of big water systems use pre–World War I technology for their water treatment, without the addition of any modern technology at all. In fact, more than eighty large public systems serving 4 million people have water that fails to meet EPA standards for filtration avoidance, yet don't have adequate filtration in place.

TABLE 3

## Basic Treatment Techniques for Public Water Supplies

| TECHNIQUE | DESCRIPTION | AGE OF TECHNIQUE |
|---|---|---|
| Sedimentation | Water is allowed to stand in protected pools to allow contaminants to settle out. | 2000 years |
| Aeration | Water is sprayed through the air, or air is bubbled through the water, to allow chemical contaminants to dissipate. | 200 years |
| Filtration | Water is passed through a bed of sand, ground coal, or other fine-particled material, which traps pathogens and contaminant particles. | 190+ years |
| Chemical Disinfection | Chlorine, ozone, or other chemicals are added to the water to kill micro-organisms. Creates disinfection by-products such as THMs unless proper preventive measures are applied. | 200+ years |
| Coagulation/ Flocculation | Chemicals added to the water and physical stirring cause contaminant particles and microorganisms to clump together, to be more easily removed by filtration and sedimentation. | 100+ years |

### Advanced Technologies

Several relatively modern methods are highly effective at removing unwanted materials from drinking water, and are even more effective when combined with pre-treatments such as coagulation, sedimentation, or filtration. Granular activated carbon, for example, can be used in municipal-size facilities to remove pathogen and chemical contaminants from water.

Membrane purification units, built with high-tech artificial filters, trap all but the very smallest particles, pathogens, and chemicals. Reverse osmosis systems are one example of a membrane-based technology.

**Clean Water Fact:** The Environmental Protection Agency has estimated that the cost of providing state-of-the-art drinking water would cost the average household less than an extra $30 per year.

## Purification Needs Vary from System to System

The treatment necessary for any particular drinking water system will depend on which contaminants may have a pathway to enter that system's water. For surface water systems with supplies coming from pristine watersheds, minimal treatment may be sufficient. Often, only rudimentary filtration is needed to reduce naturally occurring organic materials and prevent cancer-causing disinfection by-products from forming when chlorine is added.

For systems with higher levels of turbidity, coagulation and sedimentation may be needed to reduce particles that give pathogens and chemical contaminants a hiding place during treatment. For systems with water that may be periodically contaminated with chemical pollutants such as pesticides, mining wastes, or industrial solvents, granular activated carbon or membrane filtration may be needed as well. There is no one-size-fits-all cure for inadequately treated water. Unfortunately, most public water systems fail to make use of the diverse arsenal of technologies and techniques available.

## Smaller Systems Should Consolidate

For very small public water systems, even the most basic testing and analysis is prohibitively expensive, and the cost of applying modern treatment methods is unthinkable. In fact, the majority of community water systems, 50,000 in all, serve fewer than 3,300 people each. Together, these 50,000 systems provide water to barely 10 percent of the population. Often, these systems cannot afford a trained water treatment staff or even the most basic treatment technology. Combining many of these small, non-viable systems, many of which cannot meet even the most basic pathogen treatment standards, will improve the quality of the water supply to millions of people. The EPA has estimated that 50 percent of these small systems could combine with nearby larger systems to provide better water to their customers.

## IF THE ANSWERS ARE SO EASY, WHY IS THERE A PROBLEM?

If upgrading antiquated water treatment systems could solve the drinking water crisis at a cost of only $30 per household per year, you might wonder why there is still a problem.

Water utilities and state and local government agencies have claimed that they cannot afford to meet the requirements of the Safe Drinking Water Act and other environmental laws without more funding, either from the state or from Congress. They call these regulations "unfunded mandates," a complaint that also has become a rallying cry of anti-environmental extractive, industrial, and development interests across a range of issues. In 1995, Congress passed and President Clinton signed into law a measure severely restricting the government's ability to force states to bear these costs of environmental protection. The impact of this new law on drinking water quality, however, will not be known for several years.

While it is true that adequate treatment of the nation's water supply will require additional financial commitments, proposals for revolving loan funds and other innovative methods of easing the economic burden have been suggested by the federal government but have not been embraced by water utilities. Part of the cost could also be passed on to users, in their water bills or in state and local taxes; the annual amounts will generally be small, the benefit significant.

The major obstacles to improving water treatment systems

have more to do with institutional inertia and ideology than with simple budgetary constraints. Many people working within the private and the public sectors are opposed in principle to spending more money on environmental protection and public health. But spending money to protect the health of millions of Americans can hardly be viewed as a cost; it is an investment, and the savings in healthcare costs and lost wages due to illness and premature death can only be imagined. Surely they will outweigh by orders of magnitude the investment required to improve the nation's drinking water supply. Only outspoken public involvement in the policy-making process will ensure this commitment.

A detailed discussion of specific measures necessary to ensure a safe and healthy public drinking water supply, along with suggested opportunities available to consumers and voters to help make this happen, are presented in Chapter 7.

# 3

# What's in YOUR Drinking Water?

**T**here are several ways you can learn about the quality of the drinking water coming out of your tap. One good rule is to get as much information as you can, in case any one source is not testing thoroughly or reporting accurately. The several sources where you can learn about the quality of your drinking water are as follows:

- Your water company
- Your state water agency
- The Environmental Protection Agency
- Private testing laboratories

This chapter will explain how to get information from each of these sources.

## *Your Water Company*

All large water systems and most small systems are required by the Safe Drinking Water Act to test their water at regular intervals and report the results to the state and the EPA. To get a free copy of the results of these tests, call your water company. The phone number is on your water bill. Other ways to find out the phone number of your water company include:

- Looking in the phone book. If you live in a city, look up City Hall in the Government section, and call the general information number. Ask the name and number of your water company. If you live in the country, call your county government office and ask the same question.

- Calling your state water agency. Their addresses and phone numbers are listed in Appendix B.

Once you get the number of your water company, call it and explain that you are a consumer interested in learning about your drinking water. Ask to have the results of their water tests sent to you, going back two years. Some contaminant levels fluctuate seasonally, and looking at test results over a period of time lowers the possibility that you will receive only the good news.

One advantage of calling your water company is that their representative can tell you how your water is being treated. Do they use filtration? Flocculation? What kind of disinfectants do they use, and what do they do to reduce disinfection by-products? These are all good questions to ask. Most water utilities will even give you a tour of their facilities, which can help you create an informed opinion about the reliability of the information they do give you.

## Your State Water Agency

The addresses and phone numbers for every state water agency are listed in Appendix B. Call or write to your state water agency and explain that you want to learn about the quality of your drinking water. Some state agencies publish newsletters or other reports, written for consumers, that describe measures the state is taking to protect its drinking water supplies. The state can also tell you the name and number of your water company and the names and numbers of testing labs in your area, if you choose to do private testing.

## The Environmental Protection Agency

Call the EPA Safe Drinking Water Hotline. The number is

(800) 426-4791. Tell them you want to learn about your drinking water, and they will send you some useful and interesting information. They can also help you get the results of tests on your drinking water, if you haven't had success at the local or state level.

The addresses for the ten regional EPA offices are listed in Appendix C.

## Private Testing Laboratories

Having your water tested from a certified private testing laboratory will provide the most reliable information available about the water coming out of *your* tap. For one thing, any contaminants that enter the water between your water provider's treatment center and your faucet will not show up in the test results from your water provider or your state agency. These contaminants can include asbestos from asbestos-cement water mains, lead and other metals leached from service lines running from the water main to your house or building, metals leached from plumbing and fixtures within your building, and bacteria and other pathogens growing in places like your hot water tank, the water tank on the roof of your apartment house, or reservoirs between the water treatment plant and your point of use. For example, an *E. coli* outbreak that forced residents of certain New York City neighborhoods to boil their water in 1994 was attributed to bird droppings in a city reservoir.

Other reasons to consider private testing include these:

- If for any reason you don't feel confident about the information you receive from your water company

- If you have a private well or water supply and don't have a water company

- If you want more detailed or up-to-date information than your water company or the state agency can provide you

## How to Find a Reliable Testing Lab

The Environmental Protection Agency certifies labs that test drinking water. Testing can get expensive, especially if you are going to test for synthetic organic compounds (SOCs) or radiation, so get price lists from two or three labs and compare. Make sure the lab you use is EPA-certified. To find an EPA-certified lab, you have several options:

• Look in the yellow pages under Laboratories

• Call your state water agency and ask for the name of an EPA-certified lab in your area

• Call the EPA Safe Drinking Water Hotline, (800) 426-4791, and ask for the name of an EPA-certified lab in your area

If none of these options yield satisfactory results, try one of the following labs, both of which test by mail and have competitive prices:

*Suburban Water Testing*
  *Laboratories*
*4600 Kutztown Road*
*Temple, PA 19560*
*(800) 433-6595*

*National Testing Labs*
*6555 Wilson Mills Road*
*Cleveland, OH 44143*
*(800) 426-8378*

## The Problems with Testing

Even testing by a certified lab has its limitations. One problem is price. Simple lab tests can be done for $20 to $50, but comprehensive tests for ranges of chemicals or metals can easily cost more than $100. Another problem is that contaminants may vary over the course of time, and regular testing will quickly become expensive. One partial solution to the cost problem is to team up with some neighbors or even the whole neighborhood, then test the water from one home and split the bill. With the exception of metals leached from inside the house, primarily lead, the results of your neighbor's test will likely be the same as yours. For substances like asbestos, SOCs, disinfection by-products, and radiation, which typically originate before entry into the home, chances are good that anything showing up in one house will be in every house on the street.

To conclude, it is not difficult to get information about what is in your water besides water. On the other hand, to get accurate, reliable information can be more of a challenge. Ultimately, the best thing to do is get as much information as you can, then ask yourself how well you think you can trust the information you get. Some water systems, especially those of large cities, use the best in modern technology to treat their water and protect their customers. Many systems, however, fail to test or treat their water adequately, or to report their test results to the state or the EPA.

Finally, dozens of contaminants, including pesticides, residues of chemical and industrial processes, toxic metals, and even pathogens like *Cryptosporidium* are either not regulated at all or are only scheduled to be restricted at some time in the future. If you have any doubts about the quality of your drinking water, a prudent precaution would be either to purify your own water or to seek water from a more reliable source.

# The City List

This chapter contains a summary of all Safe Drinking Water Act violations reported to the EPA by the 202 largest public water systems in the United States and its territories for the years 1992 through 1994. Also included in the summary are violations reported by the two largest public water systems in ten additional states that did not make the population cutoff of the first 202; this was necessary to ensure that every state in the country was represented in the list. These 222 systems, which provide drinking water to 92 million people, reported a total of 729 violations during the time period considered.

If you live in a city served by one of these systems, you can look it up in the following pages and see whether your system reported any violations to the EPA between 1992 and 1994. This list should serve as a general guideline only: Any system that is not adequately testing or reporting its water quality could come out with "No Violations Reported" and still have bad water. If your system does show violations, however, it is a good indication that contaminants have entered your drinking water, or that your water supplier is not monitoring your water effectively enough to protect you.

The drinking water violations listed in Table 4 fall into the following categories:

- Maximum contaminant level standards violated (MCL) —indicates that actual levels for the listed contaminants exceeded federal limits on one or more occasions.

- Monitoring violation (Mon)—indicates a violation of federal requirements for monitoring and reporting the presence of the listed contaminants.

- Lead and copper rule violation (L & C)—indicates a violation of EPA standards for lead and copper testing or contamination levels.

- Surface water treatment rule violation (SWTR)—indicates a monitoring violation, a filtration requirement violation, or a violation of other unspecified treatment technique requirements.

Cities with no violations reported are listed separately in Table 6. Cities with violations involving synthetic organic chemicals (SOCs) or volatile organic chemicals (VOCs) may have these chemicals listed in Table 4, along with the other cities' violations (i.e., Louisville, KY, and Winston-Salem, NC), or, if many contaminants were involved, they may be listed separately in Table 7, with a pointer from Table 4 (i.e., Bryn Mawr, Cleveland).

The "Population" column in Table 4 indicates the population within the corresponding public drinking water system, which may be greater than the population of the indicated city, if suburbs or other nearby towns are served by the same system. Figures for cities with more than one public water system are aggregated.

Violations of the surface water treatment rule (indicated with "SWTR") can show that a city failed in its monitoring requirements (Mon) or failed to follow treatment requirements that arise when water quality reaches a particulary low level. Those violations are indicated by a "TT," for treatment technique.

Violations of the EPA's lead and copper regulations can be of three varieties:

- Initial tap sampling—a failure by a system to perform tests at household taps as required to determine if lead and copper are present in drinking water.

- Initial water quality—tap sampling was performed, but the water quality was not up to standard.

- Other—failure to meet other EPA regulations designed to prevent exposure to lead and copper in drinking water.

The contaminants listed in the City List, Table 4, are indicated by abbreviations. Table 5 (on page 47) provides the key to those abbreviations.

---

TABLE 4

## The City List: Violations of U.S. Public Drinking Water Systems, 1993–1994

| CITY | STATE | POPULATION | RULE VIOLATED | CONTAMINANTS OR VIOLATION TYPE |
|------|-------|-----------|---------------|-------------------------------|
| Aguadilla | PR | 159,876 | SWTR | Mon, TT |
| | | | Mon | Col, N |
| | | | MCL | T, Col |
| Akron | OH | 308,000 | MCL | Col |
| | | | SWTR | TT |
| Amarillo | TX | 159,000 | Mon | Col |
| Anchorage | AK | 112,535 | Mon | Ar, Ba, Cd, Cr, Col, Fl, L, M, Rad, Se, T |
| Arlington | VA | 175,000 | MCL | Col |
| Arnold | MD | 249,600 | L & C | Initial Water Quality |
| Baltimore | MD | 1,520,148 | L & C | Initial Water Quality |
| Billings | MT | 81,151 | Mon | Col |
| Boise | ID | 144,000 | Mon | Col |
| | | | MCL | Col |
| Boston | MA | 2,441,859 | SWTR | Failure to Filter |
| Boulder City | NV | 500,000 | Mon | Col |
| Bryn Mawr | PA | 783,000 | SWTR | TT |
| | | | Mon | 19 Regulated SOCs and VOCs[†] |
| Caguas | PR | 172,248 | Mon | Col |
| | | | MCL | T, Col |
| | | | SWTR | TT |
| Casper | WY | 54,500 | Mon | Col |
| Castaic | CA | 160,000 | MCL | Kepone |
| Charleston | SC | 196,752 | Mon | N, T |
| Charlotte | NC | 400,000 | SWTR | TT |

†SOCs and VOCs violations detailed in Table 7, beginning on page 49.

**TABLE 4, CONTINUED**

| CITY | STATE | POPULATION | RULE VIOLATED | CONTAMINANTS OR VIOLATION TYPE |
|------|-------|-----------|---------------|-------------------------------|
| Cheyenne | WY | 64,000 | L & C<br>Mon | Initial Tap Sampling<br>Col |
| Chicago | IL | 3,000,000 | L & C<br>Mon | Other<br>An, Be, Tm |
| Cleveland | OH | 1,428,000 | MCL<br>Mon | Col<br>39 Regulated SOCs and VOCs[†]<br>SWTR    Mon |
| Coachella | CA | 162,652 | L & C | Initial Tap Sampling |
| Colorado Springs | CO | 320,000 | SWTR | Failure to Filter |
| Columbia | SC | 248,650 | L & C<br>Mon | Initial Tap Sampling<br>N, T |
| Des Moines | IA | 193,187 | Mon | N, So |
| Detroit | MI | 1,027,974 | Mon | Col |
| Elizabeth | NJ | 576,000 | SWTR<br>Mon | Mon<br>An, N, T and 22 Regulated SOCs and VOCs[†] |
| Erie | PA | 190,000 | SWTR | TT |
| Fargo | ND | 74,111 | MCL | Col |
| Fort Wayne | IN | 180,000 | L & C<br>MCL | Initial Water Quality<br>Atrazine, Col |
| Fresno | CA | 390,350 | MCL<br>L & C | Col<br>Initial Tap Sampling, Initial Water Quality |
| Glendale | AZ | 160,000 | Mon | pH, Ar, Ba, Cd, Ca, Cl, Cr, Col, Co, Fl, I, L, Mg, Ma, M, N, pH, S, So, Su, TDS, TH, THM, Z |
| Great Falls | MT | 55,097 | Mon | Col |
| Greenville | SC | 230,555 | L & C<br>Mon<br>MCL | Initial Tap Sampling<br>Col, N, T<br>Col |
| Houston | TX | 1,576,900 | MCL | Col |
| Huntington Beach | CA | 193,000 | L & C | Initial Water Quality |
| Idaho Falls | ID | 47,300 | MCL | Col |
| Jackson | MS | 197,252 | MCL | Col |
| Jersey City | NJ | 228,537 | Mon<br>MCL<br>SWTR | Col<br>Col<br>TT, Mon |

†SOCs and VOCs violations detailed in Table 7, beginning on page 49.

**TABLE 4, CONTINUED**

| CITY | STATE | POPULATION | RULE VIOLATED | CONTAMINANTS OR VIOLATION TYPE |
|---|---|---|---|---|
| Juneau | AK | 23,965 | Mon | Ar, Ba, Coliform, Cd, Cr, Fl, L, M, N, T, S, Se, 6 Regulated SOCs and VOCs[†] |
| Kansas City | KA | 603,262 | MCL | Col |
| Las Vegas | NV | 500,000 | L & C | Initial Tap Sampling |
| | | | Mon | Col |
| Lauderdale | FL | 235,001 | Mon | Col |
| Lexington | KY | 267,300 | Mon | T |
| Little Falls | NJ | 270,000 | MCL | Col |
| | | | SWTR | Mon |
| | | | L & C | Initial Water Quality |
| | | | Mon | Ar, Ba, Cd, Coliform,Cr, Fl, L, M, N, Se, S and 22 Regulated SOCs and VOCs[†] |
| Long Beach | CA | 437,800 | L & C | Initial Tap Sampling |
| Louisville | KY | 718,182 | L & C | Other |
| | | | MCL | Col |
| | | | Mon | 2,4,5-TP (Silvex), 2,4-D, BHC-gamma (Lindane), Endrin, Methoxychlor, N, Toxaphene |
| Madison | WI | 191,262 | L & C | Initial, Follow-up, or Routine Tap Sampling |
| | | | Mon | 41 Regulated SOCs and VOCs[†] |
| Manatee County | FL | 187,501 | MCL | Col |
| Marietta | GA | 350,000 | MCL | Col |
| | | | Mon | Col |
| Mayaguez | PR | 155,720 | L & C | Initial Tap Sampling |
| | | | SWTR | Mon, TT |
| | | | Mon | Col, T |
| | | | MCL | T, Col |
| Miami | FL | 1,705,156 | L & C | Initial Tap Sampling |
| | | | Mon | Col |
| Millburn | NJ | 183,199 | L & C | Initial Water Quality |
| | | | SWTR | Mon |
| | | | Mon | An, Ar, Ba, Be, Cd, Cr, Fl, M, Ni, N, Se, So, Tm |
| Montebello | CA | 153,000 | L & C | Initial Tap Sampling, Initial Water Quality |
| Nashville | TN | 690,000 | L & C | Initial Water Quality |
| New Milford | NJ | 713,737 | L & C | Initial Water Quality, Initial Tap Sampling |

[†]SOCs and VOCs violations detailed in Table 7, beginning on page 49.

**TABLE 4, CONTINUED**

| CITY | STATE | POPULATION | RULE VIOLATED | CONTAMINANTS OR VIOLATION TYPE |
|------|-------|-----------|---------------|-------------------------------|
| New York | NY | 6,552,718 | MCL | Col, T |
| Newark | NJ | 275,221 | SWTR | TT |
| | | | Mon | An, Ar, Ba, Be, Cd, Cr, Fl, M Ni, N, Se, So, Tm |
| | | | L & C | Initial Water Quality |
| North Miami Beach | FL | 160,000 | MCL | Col |
| | | | L & C | Initial Tap Sampling, Initial Water Quality |
| Oakland | CA | 1,200,000 | L & C | Initial Water Quality |
| Oklahoma City | OK | 276,000 | SWTR | TT |
| Omaha | NE | 450,000 | L & C | Initial Water Quality |
| Pensacola | FL | 269,545 | Mon | Col |
| Peoria | IL | 158,564 | L & C | Other |
| Philadelphia | PA | 1,755,000 | L & C | Initial Water Quality |
| | | | SWTR | TT, Mon |
| Pittsburgh | PA | 1,215,543 | Mon | Col |
| | | | L & C | Initial Water Quality |
| | | | SWTR | TT, Mon |
| Ponce | PR | 216,735 | L & C | Initial Tap Sampling |
| | | | Mon | N |
| | | | SWTR | Mon, TT |
| Portland | OR | 460,000 | Mon | Col |
| Potomac | MD | 1,500,000 | L & C | Initial Tap Sampling |
| Richmond | VA | 369,000 | MCL | Col |
| Rochester | NY | 454,139 | L & C | Initial Tap Sampling |
| Salt Lake City | UT | 985,258 | Mon | Nitrite and 20 Regulated SOCs and VOCs[†] |
| San Francisco | CA | 700,000 | Mon | Col |
| San Jose | CA | 2,098,100 | L & C | Initial Water Quality |
| San Juan | PR | 1,120,536 | L & C | Initial Tap Sampling |
| | | | MCL | THM, T |
| | | | SWTR | Mon, TT |
| | | | Mon | Col, T |
| Santa Ana | CA | 293,700 | L & C | Initial Tap Sampling, Initial Water Quality |
| | | | MCL | Col |
| Scottsdale | AZ | 174,170 | MCL | Rad |
| | | | Mon | Cr, Col, THM |
| Seattle | WA | 575,600 | Mon | T |
| Shrewsbury | NJ | 302,491 | L & C | Initial Water Quality |
| | | | Mon | N |

[†]SOCs and VOCs violations detailed in Table 7, beginning on page 49.

**TABLE  4,  CONTINUED**

| CITY | STATE | POPULATION | RULE VIOLATED | CONTAMINANTS OR VIOLATION TYPE |
|------|-------|-----------|---------------|-------------------------------|
| Sioux Falls | SD | 100,814 | Mon | Col |
| St. Louis | MO | 1,637,500 | SWTR | TT |
| Syracuse | NY | 377,000 | L & C | Initial Tap Sampling |
| Tacoma | WA | 262,500 | Mon | T |
|  |  |  | Mon | T, Col |
| Tallahassee | FL | 162,750 | Mon | Col |
| Trenton | NJ | 225,000 | MCL | Cd |
|  |  |  | Mon | An, Ar, Ba, Be, Cd, Cr, Fl, M, Ni, Se, So, Tm |
|  |  |  | L & C | Initial Tap Sampling, Initial Water Quality |
| Tucson | AZ | 478,641 | MCL | Rad |
|  |  |  | Mon | Col |
| Tulsa | OK | 487,200 | SWTR | TT |
| Upland | CA | 338,660 | L & C | Initial Tap Sampling, Initial Water Quality |
| Verona | PA | 150,000 | L & C | Initial Water Quality |
| Wanaque | NJ | 200,902 | L & C | Initial Water Quality |
|  |  |  | L & C | Initial Tap Sampling, Initial Water Quality |
|  |  |  | Mon | Ar, Ba, Cd, Cr, Fl, M, N, Se |
| Washington, D.C. |  | 595,000 | MCL | Col |
| West Jordan | UT | 400,000 | Mon | Col, Nitrite |
| Winston-Salem | NC | 205,000 | Mon | 2,4,5-TP (Silvex), 2,4-D, BHC-gamma (Lindane), Endrin, Methoxychlor, Toxaphene |
| Woodbridge | NJ | 209,000 | L & C | Initial Tap Sampling, Initial Water Quality |
|  |  |  | Mon | 8 Regulated Phase I VOCs, Col, N, T |
| Worcester | MA | 175,000 | SWTR | Failure to Filter |
| Yonkers | NY | 188,082 | MCL | T |

Source: EPA-FRDS

---

TABLE 5

## Key to Contaminant Abbreviations in Table 4

| An | Antimony | L & C | Lead and Copper | Su | Sulfate |
| Ar | Arsenic | M | Mercury | T | Turbidity |
| Ba | Barium | Ma | Manganese | TDS | Total Dissolved |
| Be | Beryllium | Mon | Monitoring | | Solids |
| Ca | Calcium | Mg | Magnesium | TH | Total Hardness |
| Cd | Cadmium | Ni | Nickel | THM | Trihalomethanes |
| Cl | Chloride | N | Nitrate | Tm | Thallium |
| Co | Copper | pH | Acidity/Alkalinity | TT | Treatment |
| Col | Coliform | Rad | Alpha Radiation | | Technique |
| Cr | Chromium | S | Silver | VOCs | Volatile Organic |
| Fl | Fluoride | Se | Selenium | | Chemicals |
| I | Iron | So | Sodium | Z | Zinc |
| L | Lead | SOCs | Synthetic Organic | | |
| | | | Chemicals | | |

---

TABLE 6

## Public Water Systems Reporting No Drinking Water Violations, 1992–1994

| CITY | STATE | POP. | CITY | STATE | POP. |
|------|-------|------|------|-------|------|
| Albuquerque | NM | 417,279 | Columbus | GA | 175,000 |
| Anaheim | CA | 286,680 | Columbus | OH | 779,700 |
| Arlington | TX | 266,212 | Concord | CA | 225,000 |
| Atlanta | GA | 649,836 | Corte Madera | CA | 170,000 |
| Aurora | CO | 225,000 | Dallas | TX | 1,015,000 |
| Austin | TX | 544,336 | Dayton | OH | 150,000 |
| Baton Rouge | LA | 350,000 | Denver | CO | 1,000,000 |
| Biddeford | ME | 45,000 | Doraville | GA | 563,500 |
| Birmingham | AL | 528,000 | Durham | NC | 150,000 |
| Bridgeport | CT | 367,577 | El Paso | TX | 620,000 |
| Buffalo | NY | 748,154 | Fort Worth | TX | 477,000 |
| Buford | GA | 296,281 | Fremont | CA | 271,000 |
| Burlington | VT | 47,600 | Garland | TX | 182,861 |
| Charleston | WV | 131,913 | Gary | IN | 230,000 |
| Chula Vista | CA | 160,400 | Glendale | CA | 182,500 |
| Cincinnati | OH | 653,128 | Grand Forks | ND | 49,425 |
| Claremont | CA | 535,000 | Grand Rapids | MI | 197,649 |
| Cocoa | FL | 187,526 | Greensboro | NC | 212,000 |

**TABLE 6, CONTINUED**

| CITY | STATE | POP. | CITY | STATE | POP. |
|------|-------|------|------|-------|------|
| Haddon Heights | NJ | 210,213 | New City | NY | 225,000 |
| Halifax | MA | 203,200 | New Haven | CT | 380,000 |
| Harahan | LA | 494,441 | New Orleans | LA | 440,229 |
| Hartford | CT | 391,250 | Newark | DE | 171,800 |
| Herndon | VA | 150,000 | Newport News | VA | 350,000 |
| Honolulu | HI | 645,741 | Norfolk | VA | 295,000 |
| Huntington | WV | 76,771 | Oakdale | NY | 941,000 |
| Indianapolis | IN | 678,000 | Occoquan | VA | 550,000 |
| Irving | TX | 159,009 | Odessa | FL | 277,655 |
| Jacksonville | FL | 823,028 | Orlando | FL | 356,041 |
| Kalamazoo | MI | 150,000 | Pasadena | CA | 153,217 |
| Kansas City | MO | 450,000 | Phoenix | AZ | 1,050,000 |
| Knoxville | TN | 168,405 | Portland | ME | 109,145 |
| La Mesa | CA | 1,408,612 | Raleigh | NC | 225,000 |
| Lake Success | NY | 518,000 | Rancho | | |
| Lakeland | FL | 154,570 | Cucamonga | CA | 300,000 |
| Laredo | TX | 150,000 | Sacramento | CA | 374,600 |
| Largo | FL | 374,078 | San Antonio | TX | 963,130 |
| Lincoln | NE | 192,500 | San Jacinto | CA | 253,705 |
| Little Rock | AR | 194,629 | Savannah | GA | 154,778 |
| Los Angeles | CA | 3,600,000 | Scituate | RI | 286,923 |
| Lubbock | TX | 186,200 | Shreveport | LA | 210,000 |
| Lynbrook | NY | 238,594 | South Burlington | VT | 55,000 |
| Manchester | NH | 104,750 | Spokane | WA | 182,000 |
| Memphis | TN | 662,778 | Springfield | MA | 154,000 |
| Merrick | NY | 170,000 | St. Paul | MN | 385,000 |
| Mesa | AZ | 302,000 | Tampa | FL | 475,000 |
| Midlothian | VA | 150,000 | Toledo | OH | 388,000 |
| Milwaukee | WI | 682,332 | Va. Beach | VA | 361,024 |
| Minneapolis | MN | 473,073 | West Palm Beach | FL | 340,000 |
| Mobile | AL | 279,000 | Westlake | OH | 172,000 |
| Montgomery | AL | 220,002 | Wichita | KA | 308,058 |
| Morrow | GA | 164,081 | Youngstown | OH | 175,000 |
| Nashua | NH | 80,000 | | | |

Source: EPA-FRDS

TABLE 7

# Violations of Drinking Water Regulations for SOCs and VOCs by U.S. Public Drinking Water Systems, 1992–1994

| CITY/STATE | CONTAMINANTS |
| --- | --- |
| Bryn Mawr, PA | 1,1,2-Trichloroethane, 1,1-Dichloroethylene, 1,2,4-Trichlorobenzene, 1,2-Dichloroethane, 1,2-Dichloropropane, Benzene, Carbon Tetrachloride, cis-1,2-Dichloroethylene, Dichloromethane (Methylene Chloride), Ethylbenzene, Monochlorobenzene (Chlorobenze), o-Dichlorobenzene, p-Dichlorobenzene, Styrene, Tetrachloroethylene, Toluene, trans-1,2-Dichloroethylene, Trichloroethylene, Xylenes |
| Cleveland, OH | 2,4,5-TP (Silvex), 2,4-D, 3-Hydroxycarbofuran, Alachlor (Lasso), Aldicarb, Aldicarb Sulfone, Aldicarb Sulfoxide, Aldrin, Atrazine, Benzo(A)Pyrene, BHC-gamma (Lindane), Butachlor (Machete), Carbaryl, Carbofuran, Chlordane, Dalapon, Di (2-Ethylhexyl) Adipate, Di (2-Ethylhexyl) Phthalate, Dicamba, Dieldrin, Dinoseb, Diquat, Endothall, Endrin, Heptachlor, Heptachlor Epoxide, Hexachlorobenzene (HCB), Hexachlorocyclopentadiene, Methomyl, Methoxychlor, Metolachlor, Metribuzin (Sencor), Oxamyl (Vydate), Pentachlorophenol, Picloram, Propachlor (Ramrod), Simazine, Total Polychlorinated Biphenyl, Toxaphene |
| Elizabeth, NJ | 1,1,1-Trichloroethane, 1,1,2-Trichloroethane, 1,1-Dichloroethylene, 1,2,4-Trichlorobenzene, 1,2-Dichloroethane, 1,2-Dichloropropane, Benzene, Carbon Tetrachloride, cis-1,2-Dichloroethylene, Dichloromethane, Ethylbenzene, m-Dichlorobenzene, Monochlorobenzene, o-Dichlorobenzene, p-Dichlorobenzene, Styrene, Tetrachloroethylene, Toluene, trans-1,2-Dichloroethylene, Trichloroethylene, Vinyl Chloride, Xylenes |
| Juneau, AK | 2,4-D, 2,4,5-TP, BHC-gamma (Lindane), Endrin, Methoxychlor, Toxaphene |
| Little Falls, NJ | 1,1,1-Trichloroethane, 1,1,2-Trichloroethane, 1,1-Dichloroethylene, 1,2,4-Trichlorobenzene, 1,2-Dichloroethane, 1,2-Dichloropropane, Benzene, Carbon Tetrachloride, cis-1,2-Dichloroethylene, Dichloromethane, Ethylbenzene, m-Dichlorobenzene, Monochlorobenzene, o-Dichlorobenzene, p-Dichlorobenzene, Styrene, Tetrachloroethylene, Toluene, trans-1,2-Dichloroethylene, Trichloroethylene, Vinyl Chloride, Xylenes |

**TABLE 7, CONTINUED**

| CITY/STATE | CONTAMINANTS |
|---|---|
| Madison, WI | 1,1,1,2-Tetrachloroethane, 1,1,1-Trichloroethane, 1,1,2,2-etrachloroethane, 1,1,2-Trichloroethane, 1,1-Dichloroethane, 1,1-ichloroethylene, 1,1-Dichloropropene, 1,2,3-Trichloropropane, 1,2,4-richlorobenzene, 1,2-Dichloroethane, 1,2-Dichloropropane, 1,3-ichloropropane, 1,3-Dichloropropene, 2,2-Dichloropropane, Benzene, Bromobenzene, Bromodichloromethane, Bromoform, Bromomethane, Carbon Tetrachloride, Chloroethane, Chloroform, Chloromethane, cis-1,2-ichloroethylene, Dibromochloromethane, Dibromomethane, Dichloromethane, Ethylbenzene, m-Dichlorobenzene, Monochlorobenzene, o-Chlorotoluene, o-Dichlorobenzene, p-Chlorotoluene, p-Dichlorobenzene, Styrene, Tetrachloroethylene, Toluene, trans-1,2-Dichloroethylene, Trichloroethylene, Vinyl Chloride, Xylenes |
| Salt Lake City, UT | 1,1,1-Trichloroethane, 1,1-Dichloroethylene, 1,2,4-Trichlorobenzene, 1,2-Trichloroethane, 1,2-Dichloropropane, Benzene, Carbon Tetrachloride, cis-,2-ichloroethylene, Dichloromethane, Ethylbenzene, Monochlorobenzene, o-Dichlorobenzene, p-Dichlorobenzene, Styrene, Tetrachloroethylene, Toluene, trans-1,2-Dichloroethylene, Trichloroethylene, Vinyl Chloride, Xylenes |

Source: EPA-FRDS

# Home Treatment Systems for Unsafe Water

**A**s the previous chapters have indicated, if you use a public drinking water system, it is difficult to be confident that your water will be safe and healthy over time. Even water from pristine watersheds, if chlorinated, can carry carcinogenic disinfection by-products unless specific measures are taken to significantly reduce them at the system level. And since few systems test for *Cryptosporidium* or the many unrestricted chemicals on the EPA's priority pollutant list, some amount of uncertainty will always accompany your desire to know about your water supply.

If you have a water system that uses such advanced purification methods as granular activated carbon or reverse osmosis and you don't have to be concerned about asbestos in your water mains or lead in your plumbing or well pump, you are in the lucky minority. For the majority of Americans, relying on the water coming out of the tap is a gamble.

Fortunately, the power to protect yourself and your family is in your hands. Many options are available to ensure the safety of your drinking water supply, from purchasing water to purifying your own. This chapter explains how home water purification systems work and presents a guide to selecting good home purification equipment, if you choose to go that route. Chapter 6 explains how to purchase good water in bottles, from a home delivery service, or from vending machines.

## PURIFYING YOUR OWN

If you choose to purify your own water rather than purchasing bottled or vendor water, there are numerous alternatives available, depending on your budget and the contaminants likely to be in your water. Home units include filters, both with and without carbon; distillers; reverse osmosis units; ultraviolet (UV) systems; and cation exchange water softeners. *The purification method best for you depends on which contaminants are in your water or are most likely to get into your water in the future.* The purification devices best suited to the contaminants you wish to reduce are listed in Table 8.

TABLE 8

## Contaminants Reduced by Water Purification Devices

| PRIMARY AND SECONDARY CONTAMINANTS | CARBON FILTRATION | OTHER FILTRATION | REVERSE OSMOSIS | CATION EXCHANGE WATER SOFTENER | DISTILLATION |
|---|---|---|---|---|---|
| Arsenic | | | X | | X |
| Asbestos | | X | X | | |
| Barium | | | X | X | X |
| Cadmium | | | X | X | X |
| Chloride | | | X | | X |
| Chlorine | X | | X | | |
| Chromium | | | X | | X |
| Color | X | X | X | | |
| Copper | | | X | X | X |
| Endrin | X | | | | |
| Fluoride | | | X | | X |
| *Giardia* Cysts | | X | X | | X |
| Hardness | | | X | X | X |
| Iron (Fe²) | | X | X | X | X |
| Iron (Fe³) | | | X | | X |
| Lead | X | | X | | X |
| Lindane | X | | | | |
| Manganese | | | X | X | X |
| Mercury | | | X | | X |

**TABLE 8, CONTINUED**

| PRIMARY AND SECONDARY CONTAMINANTS | CARBON FILTRATION | OTHER FILTRATION | REVERSE OSMOSIS | CATION EXCHANGE WATER SOFTENER | DISTILLATION |
|---|---|---|---|---|---|
| | PURIFICATION METHOD | | | | |
| Methoxychlor | X | | | | |
| Nitrates | | | X | | X |
| Particulates | | X | X | | X |
| Pesticides, PCBs | X | | | | |
| Radium | | | X | X | X |
| Radon | X | | | | |
| Selenium | | | X | | X |
| Silver | | | X | | X |
| Sulfate | | | X | | X |
| THMs | X | | | | |
| Toxaphene | X | | | | |
| Turbidity | X | X | X | | X |
| VOCs | X | | | | |
| Zinc | | | X | | X |
| 2,4-D | X | | | | |
| 2,4,5-TP Silvex | X | | | | |

Source: NSF International

Once you have identified the contaminants either present or most likely to be present in your water supply, you can match the contaminants to the system or combination of systems most appropriate to your needs. Because it is often difficult to obtain reliable information about the contaminants in your water, even if you test your own water, and because those contaminants can change over time, it makes sense to get the most complete system that you can afford, one that reduces the greatest number of the commonly found drinking water contaminants, including any contaminants you know or have reason to suspect are in your water.

## Point-of-Use and Point-of-Entry Systems

Home water purification devices can be grouped into two categories: those that purify water as it enters your home or building, called point-of-entry systems, and those designed for use at a specific faucet, showerhead, or appliance, called point-of-use systems. Each one has its advantages and disadvantages.

Point-of-use systems consist of filters, reverse osmosis devices, distillation equipment, and ultraviolet purifiers. Point-of-use systems are smaller, and are less expensive to purchase and maintain, than are point-of-entry systems, but are limited to one location in a house or apartment. They are best when contaminants present a problem for drinking and cooking water.

Point-of-entry systems consist of filters, water softeners, ultraviolet disinfection systems, and aeration systems. They are comprehensive, purifying all the water entering the building, but are more costly to install and maintain than point-of-use systems. They are best with contaminants that may enter the air, such as radon or VOCs; or with contaminants that can harm appliances, plumbing, fixtures, or wash, such as hardness, iron, and copper.

## A CONSUMER'S GUIDE TO WATER PURIFIERS

The following pages group water purification devices by type and by the kinds of contaminants they reduce. Performance is based on certification by NSF International, an independent, non-profit testing organization. No government standards exist for home-use water purification devices, and the NSF ratings are considered the best standards available. NSF ratings are updated frequently; the latest copy of the NSF's rating book can be obtained by calling NSF at (313) 769-8010.

The purifier groups are divided into the following sections: water filters, including carbon and non-carbon filters; reverse osmosis systems; cation exchange water softeners;

distillers; and ultraviolet disinfection systems. For each type of purifier, the tables list manufacturer names, model numbers, and the contaminants that particular model has been certified to reduce. Manufacturer addresses and phone numbers are listed in Appendix D.

## Carbon and Non-Carbon Filters

Most filters use carbon, either in the form of carbon blocks or granular activated carbon (GAC), alone or in combination with other filtering agents. Generally, GAC is preferable because it provides greater surface area within the filter element to capture contaminants. Carbon alone will not stop *Giardia* cysts or asbestos, but combination filters will. Carbon filters are also the only purifiers to effectively reduce radon in drinking water.

Other filtering elements include porous ceramics and synthetic fibers. Water flows through or across the filtering agent, and contaminants are captured by the filter element. As contaminants build up, it is necessary to change the filter. Failure to do so can result in water that is worse than the water that comes out of the tap, as built-up contaminants flush into the outflow. For this reason, *be sure to replace filter elements at least as often as the manufacturer specifies.*

The Most Comprehensive Filters category in the filter listings contains filters that reduce the most commonly found drinking water contaminants, including asbestos, lead, cysts, THMs and VOCs. Filters in other categories reduce successively fewer contaminants but, depending on your filtering needs, they may be fine for you. In addition to reducing contaminants that pose health dangers, many of the listed filters are also designated as either "aesthetic Class I" or "aesthetic Class II" certified. These designations indicate a certification rating as either the best or second best, respectively, for reducing chlorine and non–health-threatening contaminants that can give drinking water a bad taste or odor.

## Airborne Radon

Radon is not only a drinking water contaminant, but can enter the air of your home from the ground below. In fact, the EPA believes radon is the second leading cause of lung cancer in the United States after cigarette smoke. Airborne radon test kits for the home can be purchased at most hardware stores for about $10.

As with purifiers in general, the filter that is best for you will depend on which specific contaminants you have in your water. Filters not listed in the following tables were not certified by NSF as of June 1995.

## THE MOST COMPREHENSIVE FILTERS

Among the drinking water filters certified by NSF International, the filters listed in Table 9 reduced the broadest range of the most important contaminants. They all reduce more than five contaminants, including asbestos, cysts, lead, THMs, and VOCs, and all received a Class I rating for aesthetic filtration as well.

TABLE 9

**Filters Certified to Reduce 5 or More Contaminants from Drinking Water, Including Asbestos, Cysts, Lead, THMs, and VOCs**

Key:

1   Amway (Japan) LTD, Model E-8301-J

2   Amway Corporation (USA), Models WTS E-9225/E9229, 9233, WTS E-84/E-86, E-8301-J

3   Diamite Corp. System 1720

4   Liberty Drinking Water Systems, Models DWS-U/C, DWS-I/L, DWS-C/T

5   Multi-Pure Drinking Water Systems, Models MPC 500B, MPC 500I, MPC 500C, MPC 250, 500 FBC, MP-SSCT, MPC 900, 500 FBB, 500 FBI

6   Rainsoft Water Conditioning Company, Models Hydrefiner 9878, Hydrefiner 9879

**TABLE 9, CONTINUED**

| CONTAMINANTS REDUCED | FILTER NUMBER | | | | | |
|---|---|---|---|---|---|---|
| | 1 | 2 | 3 | 4 | 5 | 6 |
| Alachlor | X | X | | | | |
| Asbestos | X | X | X | X | X | X |
| Atrazine | X | X | | | | |
| Chlordane | X | X | | | | |
| Cysts | X | X | X | X | X | X |
| DBC | | X | | | | |
| Ethylene Dibromide | | X | | | | |
| Heptachlorepoxide | X | X | | | | |
| Lead | X | X | X | X | X | X |
| Lindane | X | X | X | X | X | X |
| Mercury | X | X | | | | |
| Methoxychlor | X | X | | | | |
| PCB | X | X | | | | |
| Toxaphene | X | X | | | | |
| Trihalomethanes | X | X | X | X | X | X |
| Turbidity | X | X | X | X | X | X |
| VOC | X | X | X | X | X | X |
| Xylene | X | X | | | | |
| 2,4,5-TP | X | X | | | | |
| 2,4-D | X | X | X | X | X | X |
| Aesthetic Class I | X | X | X | X | X | X |

Abbreviations:
DBC    Dibromochloropropane          PCB    Polychlorinated bi-phenols
VOC    Volatile Organic Chemicals

Source: NSF International

## THE SECOND-MOST-COMPREHENSIVE FILTERS

The filters listed in Table 10 reduce five or more contaminants, but not each of asbestos, lead, cysts, THMs, and VOCs. Each one also received the highest rating for removing bad taste and odor.

TABLE 10

## Filters Certified to Reduce 5 or More Contaminants from Drinking Water, *Not* Necessarily Including Asbestos, Cysts, Lead, THMs, and VOCs

*Key:*

1  Amway Corporation (USA), Models Compact E-9395/E-9397+

2  Diamite Corp., System 1710

3  Everpure, Inc., Models Breakmate Premium, Standguard XP1, XP2, S-200, Preferred Series 350, ProSeries 3500, QC4-VOC

4  Everpure, Inc., Models H-200, QL2-OW200L, BW-500, OC4-THM System

5  Hy Cite Corp., Models Infinity I 500RP, Infinity II 600RP

6  Neo-Life Company of America, Water Dome Model #28, Water Dome Model #29, Water Dome Model #32

7  Regal Ware Inc., Models K6795ASF, K6795JA, K6795BSF, K6795JB

8  Water Factory Systems, Inc., Models CM3-3C, FM3-3C, CM3-3CM, FM3-3CM

| CONTAMINANT REDUCED | FILTER NUMBER | | | | | | | |
|---|---|---|---|---|---|---|---|---|
| | 1 | 2 | 3 | 4 | 5 | 6 | 7 | 8 |
| Asbestos | | | X | X | | | | |
| Cysts | X | X | X | X | X | X | X | X |
| Lead | X | | X | X | | | X | X |
| Lindane | | X | | | X | X | | |
| Turbidity | X | X | X | X | X | X | X | X |
| Trihalomethanes | X | X | | X | X | X | | X |
| Toxaphene | | | | | | | X | |
| VOCs | X | X | X | | X | X | X | X |
| 245 | | | | | | | X | |
| Aesthetic Class I | X | X | X | X | X | X | X | X |

Abbreviations:    VOC    Volatile Organic Chemicals

Source: NSF International

The filters listed in Table 11 each reduce four contaminants from drinking water, and received either the highest or the second-highest rating for reducing bad taste and odor.

---

TABLE 11

## Filters Certified to Reduce 4 Contaminants from Drinking Water

*Key:*

1 Everpure, Inc., Models Oceanus Supreme, US2000, QC4-THM/SC, QC4-VOC System

2 Everpure, Inc., Models H-50, BW-400, S-54

3 Water Factory Systems, Inc., Models CM3-3A, FM3-3A CM3-3AM, FM3-3AM

4 Water Factory Systems, Inc., Models CM3-3B, FM3-3B CM3-3BM, FM3-3BM

5 Watts Regulator Co., Models WFS-200 WF-VOC

6 Whirlpool Corporation, Model WSC300YW

| CONTAMINANT REDUCED | FILTER NUMBER | | | | | |
|---|---|---|---|---|---|---|
| | 1 | 2 | 3 | 4 | 5 | 6 |
| Asbestos | X | X | | | | |
| Cysts | X | X | X | X | X | X |
| Lead | | X | X | X | X | X |
| Turbidity | X | X | X | X | X | X |
| Trihalomethanes | X | | | X | | |
| VOC | | | X | | X | X |
| Aesthetic Class I | X | X | | | X | |
| Aesthetic Class II | | | | X | | X |

Source: NSF International

## LESS-COMPREHENSIVE FILTERS

The filters listed in Table 12 reduce three or fewer contaminants from drinking water. Some of them also received either a Class I or a Class II rating for reducing bad taste and odor.

TABLE 12

## Filters Certified to Reduce 3 or Fewer Contaminants from Drinking Water

| MAKE AND MODEL | CONTAMINANTS REDUCED |
|---|---|
| A.H.P. Inc., Model CTN-710 | T, AE1 |
| Brita, Models OB01/OB03 Standard, OB13/OB03 Ultra II, OB01/OB07 Standard, OB13/OB07 Ultra II, OB11/OB03 Slim, OB11/OB07 Slim | L, Co |
| Culligan Int'l, System 301 | VOC |
| Cuno, Inc., Model Aqua-Pure AP CRF | VOC |
| Cuno, Inc., Model Aqua-Pure AP26T | Cy, T |
| Cuno, Inc., Models CFS8571/CFS8111, CFS8571-S/CFS8111-S | T, AE1 |
| Cuno, Inc., Models CFS-BCI-1, 2, 3, CFS01/CFS2501, CFS02/CFS2502, CFS11/CFS2501, CFS12/CFS2502, CFS12/CFS8001-2M | Cy, T |
| Doulton Water Filters, Model HIP/Carbosyl | Cy, T, AE1 |
| Doulton Water Filters, Model HIP/Sterasyl | T |
| Everpure, Inc., Models Culligan 1, QC71-TO | THM |
| Everpure, Inc., Models QC2-AC, QC71-XC, QC4-C, QC71-3000, OC4-H, QC71-2000, QC7-MC, QC4-BH, QC7, I-MC, QL2-OCS, QC7-MH, H-100, QC7-XC, MD-HN, MD-CN, MD-CE, MD-HE, GA, 3000-2DC, BW-100, Standguard PF, Culligan 2, Insurice 2000, 3000 Scotsman SSM, Nu Life CT-500, Oceanus 750, Oceanus 0-750, ProSeries 1500 and 2500, Preferred Series 150 and 250, HF Filter, Breakmate Fine S-100 System | As, Cy, T, AE1 |
| Filtercold Corp., Models CT-N, Av-50, Av-80 | T, AE1 |
| Kinetico Inc., MAC model 5500, 6500 | L, T, VOC |
| Rainsoft Water Conditioning Company, Model Hydrefiner 9765; Model Leadex 9860 | T, Cy, L, AE1 |
| Selecto, Inc., LeadOUT Model 10 | L |
| Selecto, Inc., Model SP MF | T |
| Selecto, Inc., Model Supra Plus 30 | T |
| Teledyne Water Pik, Model Instapure IF-10A | Li |
| Teledyne Water Pik, Model Instapure IF-100A | L, Li |

| | | | | | |
|---|---|---|---|---|---|
| As | Asbestos | Co | Copper | Cy | Cysts |
| L | Lead | T | Turbidity | Li | Lindane |
| THM | Trihalomethanes | VOC | Volatile Organic Chemicals | | |
| AE1 | Aesthetic Effects, Class I | AE2 | Aesthetic Effects, Class II | | |

**TABLE  12,  CONTINUED**

| MAKE AND MODEL | CONTAMINANTS REDUCED |
|---|---|
| Ultra-Flo Systems, Models UF-4001, UF-6001 | T, AE1 |
| Water Factory Systems, Inc., Models CM1-1A, FM1-1A, CM2-1A, FM2-1A, CM2-1B, FM2-1B, CM3-1A, FM3-1A, CM3-1B, FM3-1B | T, AE2 |
| Water Factory Systems, Inc., Models CM2-3A, FM2-3A, CM2-4A, FM2-4A | L, AE2 |
| Water Factory Systems, Inc., Models CM2-3B, FM2-3B, CM2-3BM, FM2-3BM | Cy, L, T, AE2 |
| Water Factory Systems, Inc., Models CM3-2B, FM3-2B, CM3-2BM, FM3-2BM | Cy, THM, T, AE2 |
| Watts Regulator Co., Models WF-100, WFS-100 | T, Cy, AE1 |
| Watts Regulator Co., Model WF-200 | T, Cy, THM, AE1 |
| Watts Regulator Co., Model WF-THM | T, Cy, THM, AE1 |
| Whirlpool Corporation, Model WSC200YW | Cy, L, T, AE2 |

| As | Asbestos | Co | Copper | Cy | Cysts |
|---|---|---|---|---|---|
| L | Lead | T | Turbidity | Li | Lindane |
| THM | Trihalomethanes | VOC | Volatile Organic Chemicals | | |
| AE1 | Aesthetic Effects, Class I | AE2 | Aesthetic Effects, Class II | | |

Source: NSF International

## Reverse Osmosis Systems

Reverse osmosis (RO) systems reduce contaminants by pushing water up against a membrane that stops contaminants from passing but allows water to get through.  Unlike filters, which trap contaminants in their elements, RO systems flush away most of the impurities with wastewater that does not make it through the membrane.  For this reason, RO systems "use" more water than they produce, a negative in areas of drought or water shortage.  Like filtration systems, RO systems need to have their membranes replaced periodically due to wear and accumulation of contaminants.

As Table 8 indicates, RO systems are highly effective at reducing a broad range of contaminants, much more effective than filtration alone. RO systems reduce all metals, many pesticides, and asbestos, but they will not remove lighter molecules like THMs, radon, and VOCs, or pesticides such as lindane and atrazine. To compensate for these weaknesses, many RO systems come with carbon filtration units added on.

Table 13 lists reverse osmosis systems certified by NSF for the listed contaminants as of June 1995.

**TABLE 13**

## Reverse Osmosis Systems
## Certified for Drinking Water Purification

| MAKE AND MODEL | CONTAMINANTS REDUCED |
|---|---|
| Aqua Care Systems, Revos Series | Ar, Ba, Cd, Ch(H), Ch(T), Fl, L, M, R, Se, TDS |
| Culligan International, H-83, H-83SC, H-83C-Remote, H-83SC Premier, H-83 PRV-C | Ar, As, Ba, Cd, Ch(H), Ch(T), Fl, L, M, R, Se, TDS |
| Culligan International , H-83SC Nitrate, H-83C Nitrate Ch(H), Ch(T), N, Fl, L, M, R, Se, TDS | Ar, As, Ba, Cd, |
| Ecodyne, 625.34 7050, Northstar, Tapworks | TDS only |
| Ecowater Systems, Eco Elite ERO494E | TDS only |
| Everpure, Inc. , Ultimate 1, ROM II, ROM III | Ba, Cd, Ch(H), Ch(T), Fl, L, M, N, S |
| Hydrotechnology, Inc. F-HT-9A, F-HT-15A, F-HT-9, F-HT-15, F-HT-25, F-HT-35, F-HT-45, F-HTF-9, F-HTF-15, F-HTF-25, F-HTF-35, F-HTF-45 | TDS, Ba, Ch(H), FL, M, Cd, L, Cy, T |
| Kinetico, Inc., Model 516, Model 517, Model 518, Model 519 | Ar, Ba, Cd, Ch(H), Ch(T), Cy, Fl, L, M, R, Se, TDS, T, VOC |
| Kinetico, Inc., Model 517N | Ar, Ba, Cd, Ch(H), Ch(T), Cy, Fl, L, M, N, R, Se, TDS, T, VOC |
| Kinetico, Inc., Model 520, Model 521 | Ba, Cd, Ch(H), Ch(T), Cy, Fl, L, M, R, Se, TDS, T, VOC |
| Kiss International, Aristocrat I, Aristocrat III | Ar, Fl, L, TDS |

Abbreviations:
| | | | | | |
|---|---|---|---|---|---|
| Ar | Arsenic | CH(H) | Hexavalent Chromium | M | Mercury |
| As | Asbestos | CH(T) | Trivalent Chromium | N | Nitrate |
| Ba | Barium | Cy | Cysts | R | Radium |
| Ca | Calcium | Fl | Fluoride | Se | Selenium |
| Cd | Cadmium | L | Lead | T | Turbidity |
| TDS | Total Dissolved Solids | | VOC Volatile Organic Chemicals | | |

**TABLE 13, CONTINUED**

| MAKE AND MODEL | CONTAMINANTS REDUCED |
|---|---|
| Kiss International, Aristocrat I N, Aristocrat III N | Ar, Fl, L, N, TDS |
| Rainsoft Water Conditioning Company, Ultrefiner 9590 | Fl, L, Ch(H), Ch(T), M, Se, TDS |
| Rainsoft Water Conditioning Company, Ultrefiner 9591, Ultrefiner 9596 | Ar, Fl, Ch(H), Ch(T), L, M, S, T, TDS |
| Rainsoft Water Conditioning Company, Ultrefiner 9591N, Ultrefiner 9596N | Ar, Fl, Ch(H), Ch(T), L, M, N, S, T, TDS |
| Shaklee Corporation, BestWater 50800, | As, Ba, Ch(H), Ch(T), Cy, Fl, M, R, Se, T, TDS, VOC |
| Shaklee Corporation, BestWater 51000 | Ar, As, Ba, Cd, Ch(H), Ch(T), Cy, Fl, L, M, R, Se, T, TDS, VOC |
| Shaklee Corporation, BestWater 50805 | As, Ba, Ch(H), Ch(T), Cy, Fl, M, R, Se, T, TDS |
| Sears, See Ecodyne | |
| The Water Exchange, Geolait 5 | Ar, Ba, Ca, Ch(H), Ch(T), Fl, L, M, R, Se, TDS |
| Water Factory Systems, Inc., N4000 CTA SO, Grainger RO5000 | Ba, Cd, Fl, Ch(H), Ch(T), L, M, R, Se, TDS |
| Water Factory Systems, Inc., N4000 TFCM SO, N5000 TFCM SO, N4500 TFCM SO, SQC2 Series, SQC3 Series, SQC4 Series, SQC4 Plus Series, APRO 5000, CMTRO-3TFC, CMTRO-4TFC, CMRO-3TFC, CMRO-4TFC | Ar, Ba, Cd, Fl, Ch(H), Ch(T), L, M, R, Se, TDS |
| Water Factory Systems, Inc., N4000 TFCM SO Nitrate, SQC2 Nitrate Series, SQC3 Nitrate Series, SQC4 Nitrate Plus | Ar, Ba, Cd, Fl, Ch(H), Ch(T), L, M, N, R, Se, TDS |
| Water Factory Systems, Inc., SQC1 Series, CMTRO-3CTA, CMRO-3CTA, G.I.1, G.I.1 | As, Ba, Cd, Cy, Fl, Ch(H), L, M, R, Se, T, TDS |
| Water Resources International, WRI Super Deluxe-C | Ar, Ba, Cd, Cy, L, N, R, T, TDS, VOC |

Abbreviations:

| | | | | | |
|---|---|---|---|---|---|
| Ar | Arsenic | CH(H) | Hexavalent Chromium | M | Mercury |
| As | Asbestos | CH(T) | Trivalent Chromium | N | Nitrate |
| Ba | Barium | Cy | Cysts | R | Radium |
| Ca | Calcium | Fl | Fluoride | Se | Selenium |
| Cd | Cadmium | L | Lead | T | Turbidity |
| TDS | Total Dissolved Solids | | VOC Volatile Organic Chemicals | | |

**TABLE 13, CONTINUED**

| MAKE AND MODEL | CONTAMINANTS REDUCED |
|---|---|
| Water Resources International, WRI-Ultra Micron Filtration-A, WRI Super Deluxe-A, TRK-V-Royal Knight-A, AQUA-IV-Super Deluxe-A | TDS, VOC only |
| Water Resources International, WRI-Ultra Micron, Filtration-B, WRI Super Deluxe, TRK-V-Royal Knight-B, AQUA-IV-Super Deluxe-A | Ar, Ba, Cd, Cy, L, M, R T, TDS, VOC |
| Water Resources International, WRI-Ultra Micron Filtration-C, WRI Super Deluxe-B, TRK-V-Royal Knight-C, AQUA-IV-Super Deluxe-A | Ar, Ba, Cd, Cy, L, M, N, R T, TDS, VOC |
| Watercare Corporation, Ultrowater II-1, Ultrowater II-2 | Ar, Ba, Cd, Ch(H), Ch(T), Fl, L, M, R, Se, TDS |
| Watercare Corporation, Ultrowater II-3 | Ar, Ba, Cd, Ch(H), Ch(T), Fl, L, M, N, R, Se, TDS |
| Whirlpool Corporation, WSR413YW | Ar, Ba, Cd, Ch(H), Ch(T), Fl, L, M, N, R, Se, TDS |

Abbreviations:

| | | | | | |
|---|---|---|---|---|---|
| Ar | Arsenic | CH(H) | Hexavalent Chromium | M | Mercury |
| As | Asbestos | CH(T) | Trivalent Chromium | N | Nitrate |
| Ba | Barium | Cy | Cysts | R | Radium |
| Ca | Calcium | Fl | Fluoride | Se | Selenium |
| Cd | Cadmium | L | Lead | T | Turbidity |
| TDS | Total Dissolved Solids | | VOC  Volatile Organic Chemicals | | |

Source: NSF International

## Cation Exchange Water Softeners

"Hardness" in water is caused by the presence of calcium and magnesium, which lessen the effectiveness of soaps and detergents and can produce scale in pipes, hot water tanks, and appliances. Cation exchange water softeners replace the calcium and magnesium in water with sodium, which doesn't have the negative effects associated with hardness. Water softeners also reduce certain contaminants from water and therefore can have some benefit as purification devices, although as Table 14 shows, that benefit is limited compared to reverse osmosis or filtration systems.

The arguments in favor of softening water tend to be economic ones—over time hard water may clog pipes, cause appliances to age prematurely, and require more soap for cleaning. Claims that hard water causes kidney stones and other ailments are poorly supported by scientific and medical literature. On the other hand, hard water provides an important source of dietary calcium, which is essential to promoting strong bones and teeth and to preventing osteoporosis. Also, a growing body of evidence indicates that hard water significantly lowers your chances of arteriosclerosis and other forms of cardiovascular disease. Finally, water softeners increase water's corrosivity, which can accelerate the leaching of lead and other toxic metals from pipes and fixtures.

The best solution, if you have hard water, is to install point-of-use systems for your appliances but not for your drinking water.

Table 14 lists the cation exchange water softeners certified by NSF for softener performance or reduction of the indicated contaminants as of June 1995.

## TABLE 14

## Cation Exchange Water Softeners Certified for Drinking Water Purification

| MAKE AND MODEL | CONTAMINANTS REDUCED |
|---|---|
| Chemical Engineering Corporation, MacCLEAN and AQUATEK models NS0500, NS0501, NS1500, NS1501, NS2500, NS2501, NSM0750, NSM0751, NSM1000, NSM1001, NSM1500, NSM1501, NSM2000, NSM2001, NSM2500, NSM2501, NLS0500, NLS0501, NLS0750, NLS0751, NLS1000, NLS1001, NLSM0750, NLSM0751, NLSM1000, NLSM1001 | SP |
| Chemical Engineering Corporation, MacCLEAN and AQUATEK models, NS0750, NS0751, NS1000, NS1001, NS2000, NS2001 | SP, I |
| Culligan International Company, Mark 812 Aqua-Sensor, Mark 89 Aqua-Sensor | SP, B, Ra |

Abbreviations:
B  Barium      I   Iron      Ra  Radium 226/228      SP   Softener Performance

**TABLE 14, CONTINUED**

| MAKE AND MODEL | CONTAMINANTS REDUCED |
|---|---|
| Culligan International Company, Mark 512 Aqua-Sensor, Mark 812, Mark 812 Soft-Minder, N8 Custom 00401117, Mark 512, Mark 89, Mark 89 Soft-Minder, Mark 59, Mark 59 Aqua-Sensor | SP |
| Cuno, Inc., NWSC050, NWSC075, NWSC100, NWS050, NWS075, NWS100, NWS150, NWS200, NWS250, NWS075M, NWS100M, NWS150M, NWS200M, NWS250M, NWSC075M, NWSC100M | SP |
| Kinetico Incorporated, Model Numbers 25, 30, 60, 100A, 50C, 50, 51 | SP, Ba, Ra |

Abbreviations:
B  Barium      I   Iron       Ra  Radium 226/228      SP   Softener Performance

Source: NSF International

## Distillation Systems

The risks and benefits of drinking distilled water are the subject of significant debate in the scientific and medical communities, without a clear consensus on either side. Distillation reduces turbidity and the presence of many harmful contaminants from water, including all metals and nitrates, and distillation kills bacteria, viruses, and cysts. Distillation does not remove asbestos, chlorine, THMs, or most pesticides and VOCs.

But distillation softens water, removing calcium and magnesium, nutrients essential to human health, as discussed in the previous section on water softeners. Distilled water also dissolves materials more readily than non-distilled water, a quality referred to as "aggressiveness." Aggressive distilled water will leach toxins from plastic containers, for example, much more rapidly than other types of purified water will.

As of January 1995, no distillation systems were certified by NSF International, although NSF had established a testing standard at that time. To find out if NSF has certified any distillation systems as of the present date, call them at (313) 769-8010.

In 1990, *Consumer Reports* magazine tested five home water distillers. Of the five tested, two models stood out as superior. They are the Aqua Clean MD-4 and the Sears Cat. No. 34555. For more information about those two products, contact the manufacturers at:

*Sears Roebuck & Company*          *Aqua Clean*
*Sears Tower*                               *Pure Water Inc.*
*233 S. Wacker Dr.*                      *P.O. Box 83226*
*Chicago, IL 60606*                      *Lincoln, NE 68501*
*(800) 366-3000*                         *(800) 875-5915*

## Ultraviolet Disinfection Systems

Ultraviolet (UV) light is highly effective at killing microorganisms in drinking water, provided there is not too much turbidity, nor are there too many suspended particles, both of which give pathogens a place to hide. If you have well water with pathogen contamination that cannot be identified and removed at the source, an ultraviolet system may be the solution. UV systems work by passing the water through a chamber that is inundated with ultraviolet light. Good systems have sensors with shut-off switches or alarms that go off when UV levels drop below those necessary for disinfection. For water with high turbidity, a pre-filter should be used to reduce particles that can lower the UV system's effectiveness.

As of June 1995, only one model of UV device was certified by NSF International: the Amway Model E-8301-J, which received a Class B disinfection performance rating.

**6**

○

# Buying Safe Water

If you choose to purchase water from a source other than the one hooked up to your faucets, you have two options: bottled water and vending machine water. Vending machine water has the advantage of low cost, typically running twenty-five to fifty cents a gallon, while bottled water can cost a dollar a gallon, or more. Bottled water has the advantage of convenience, since you can have it delivered to your home or office. In terms of reliability, either option can provide you with a quality source of good-tasting, healthy drinking water, if you are a careful consumer.

## VENDOR WATER

With increasing public concern about drinking water quality, a new industry has sprung up to put water vending machines in grocery stores and other convenient outlets. These machines require you to supply your own container, although stores with the machines often sell various sizes of plastic water containers as well.

Vendor water can vary considerably in quality, depending on the machine and the quality of the source water used. Most water vending machines in stores are hooked up directly to the plumbing in the building, and therefore to the municipal water supply. The water is then processed, either through a filter or a series of treatments. Some models process water through a granular activated carbon filter, through a reverse osmosis purifier, and then through an ultraviolet disinfector. This is better purification than most homeowners are likely to install in their own kitchens. If you are considering buying water from a vending machine, look to see if the kind of treatment it provides is described on the machine itself. If not, ask someone in the store.

One problem with vending machine water is that as a consumer you have no way to determine if the equipment is properly maintained. In fact, vendor water is not regulated at all. Glacier Water Services, the biggest water vending machine operator in the United States, claims its machines sell up to 81 gallons of water a day in large supermarkets. This amounts to more than 29,000 gallons a year through a single machine, which means potential problems if filters and other elements are not serviced on a regular basis. As of this writing, there is no national standard or certification for water vending machines, so you have to judge for yourself whether you can trust the store that is operating the machine to maintain it properly.

## BOTTLED WATER

Bottled water comes in two major product categories, specialty water, which comes in small bottles and competes with soft drinks and bottled juices, and bulk water, which comes in large containers, is not carbonated, and is used for cooking and day-to-day drinking water. Bulk water can be ordered for home delivery in many parts of the country.

The Food and Drug Administration (FDA) sets standards for bottled water sold through interstate commerce in the United States. Beginning in 1995, those standards were set to match the maximum contaminant level requirements for municipal water systems under the Safe Drinking Water Act. Individual states are solely responsible for the regulation of bottled water produced and sold within their own borders, but can set their own higher standards for water that is also regulated by the FDA. Many states have chosen to set higher standards than those of the federal government.

Producers of both specialty water and bulk water can become members of the International Bottled Water Association (IBWA), which maintains quality control measures for the products and bottling processes of its members. IBWA members' bottling facilities are subject to random inspection and testing, and must meet standards that historically have been higher than those set by the FDA. Also, some water bottlers have chosen to obtain certification of their product from NSF International, the independent, non-profit testing and certification organization whose findings were used to rate water purifiers in Chapter 5. All products certified by NSF, like the products of IBWA members, have met or exceeded standards required for municipal drinking water.

If you do choose to purchase bottled water as your primary source of drinking water, at the very least you should buy from a bottler who is either a member of the IBWA or has been NSF-certified. In addition, ask the bottler how often their water is tested, and ask for a copy of the test results. Water from a company that uses an independent laboratory to do its testing is presumably more reliable than water from a bottler that only does its own testing.

## Advantages and Disadvantages of Bottled Water

Compared to tap water, bottled water has both advantages and disadvantages. The biggest disadvantage of bottled water is cost. Bottled water, either from the store or from a home delivery service, can cost a dollar a gallon or more, while tap water generally costs a few cents a gallon in most water systems. Adding in the cost of a home purification system still typically leaves the per-gallon cost of tap water below twenty cents. Another disadvantage of bottled water is that unless you are vigilant about the source, you may be buying unreliably treated tap water; you could treat tap water yourself for a much lower cost. According to the International Bottled Water Association, up to 25 percent of bottled water in the

United States consists of municipal water that has been treated in some way, but whose treatment is completely unregulated.

Bottled water does have advantages over untreated tap water. Even bottlers who use municipal water for their source often use excellent purification technology and constantly test and monitor their product. Many water bottlers use ozone for disinfection rather than chlorine; ozone is less likely to create disinfection by-products than chlorine.

Another advantage of bottled water is that it is not exposed to contaminants such as lead and asbestos, which may be present in the distribution system of municipal supplies between the treatment plant and your home or apartment. Finally, in the event of an emergency such as a waterborne disease outbreak from a municipal system, bottled water may be the only alternative until public supplies are restored.

## Plastic Bottles

A final disadvantage of bottled water is the container itself. Plastic can leach phthalates and other chemicals, many of which have not been thoroughly tested for toxicity, into the water. Two types of plastic are commonly used for bottled water, polyethylene and polycarbonate. Polyethylene is the cloudier looking, softer type of plastic. Polycarbonate is a clearer, harder, more brittle plastic. Polyethylene tends to give water more of a "plastic" taste, especially after exposure to direct sunlight or after long storage periods. This may indicate the presence of chemical contaminants.

If you do buy water in plastic bottles, treat it as you would a food product: Don't leave it in the sun, don't store it for excessively long periods of time, and don't leave containers open when they are not in use. Also, the longer a bottle of water has been open, the greater the chances of bacterial growth and other types of contamination.

Another problem with plastic bottles, regardless of chem-

ical leaching, is the very fact that they are plastic. The production of plastic uses petrochemicals and creates the very
kind of pollution that is threatening our water supplies to
begin with. Also, plastic is not usually biodegradable, and
"recycled" plastic either gets shipped to developing countries
for disposal in landfills or, occasionally, gets one more round
of use as filling in winter jackets or park benches before getting buried in the earth. This problem is greater with store-
bought water than delivered water, which comes in reusable
containers.

## Mineral Water, Spring Water, and Other Labels

A momentary glance at the many varieties of bottled water filling grocery store shelves is enough to confuse even the most
discriminating shopper. The bottled water business has grown
to a $2.5 billion a year industry in the United States, with close
to a thousand bottlers vying for customer loyalty. The variety
of brand names and product types can be daunting.

In response to confusion by consumers and sometimes
deceptive labeling by bottlers, in 1995 the Food and Drug
Administration established the following definitions for various types of bottled water.

- **Mineral water** comes from a source tapped at one or
  more bore holes or springs originating from a geologi-
  cally or physically protected underground water
  source and containing at least 250 parts per million of
  total dissolved solids.

- **Spring water** is derived from an underground formation from which water naturally flows to the surface of
  the earth, or would flow to the surface of the earth if
  not for its collection below the earth's surface. This
  definition allows for wells or bore holes tapped next
  to the natural point of emergence.

- **Artesian water** is drawn from a well tapping a confined aquifer that has a water level above the natural

water table in the area, indicating that the water was under pressure.

- **Purified water** is produced by distillation, deionization, reverse osmosis, or "other suitable processes" and meets the definition of "purified water" in the most recent edition of the *U.S. Pharmacopœia*, which lists the standards of the U.S. pharmaceuticals industry.

- **Distilled water** meets the definition of purified water and is produced by distillation.

- **Well water** is bottled water from a hole bored in the ground that taps water from an aquifer.

- **Nursery water** or infant drinking water was sometimes deceptively labeled to indicate suitability for baby formula mixes without having been sterilized by boiling or by any other means. The 1995 FDA rules require all water bottled with such a label to state clearly that it is not sterile, unless the water has been treated to make it sterile and to maintain its sterility throughout its shelf life.

In addition to these definitions, the FDA established labeling requirements to prevent a seller of purified (or unpurified) municipal water, from depicting a mountain stream or a natural spring on its product label, falsely implying that the water in the bottle came from such a source.

## How to Choose a Bottled Water

In a 1991 study by the University of Iowa, thirty-nine samples of bottled water were analyzed for the presence of contaminants. Of those thirty-nine samples, eleven contained measurable levels of trihalomethanes (THMs), eighteen contained nitrates, and others contained traces of arsenic, barium, and toluene. Some also contained significant levels of bacteria. The conclusion of the Iowa study was that the bottled water was not significantly better or worse than the public drinking water in the state. If you are going to purchase bottled water, make sure you are getting what you pay for. Buy water from an NSF-certified bottler, or a member of the International Bottled Water Association (IBWA).

The IBWA has more than 700 member bottlers, far too many to list here. Many popular brands of carbonated bottled water, such as Perrier and Calistoga, are not included in the NSF listings but are certified by the IBWA. To check if a brand you are interested in is produced by an IBWA member, for free information about specific bottlers, or for information about IBWA bottlers in your region, call the IBWA toll free at (800) 928-3711.

Table 15 lists the names of bottlers, brands, and products for all bottled water certified by NSF International as of 1995. Brands are certified only for the container sizes indicated in the right-hand column of the listing table. For more up-to-date listings, contact NSF at (313) 769-8010.

TABLE 15

## Bottled Water Certified by NSF International as of March 1994

| TRADE NAME/PRODUCT TYPE | MANUFACTURER | SIZE* |
|---|---|---|
| Acme / Spring Water | Ephrata Diamond Spring Water Co. | 1 |
| Alhambra / Crystal Fresh Water | McKesson Water Products Company | 1, 3, 5, 2.5 |
| Alhambra / Fluoridated Drinking Water | McKesson Water Products Company | 3, 5 |
| Alhambra / Purified Water | McKesson Water Products Company | 1, 3, 5, 2.5 |
| AquaPenn / Distilled Water | AquaPenn Spring Water Company | 1, 5, 2.5 |
| AquaPenn / Spring Water | AquaPenn Spring Water Company | 1, 2.5, 5, 1, 1.5 L,12, 16 oz. |
| AquaPenn / Spring Water With Fluoride | AquaPenn Spring Water Company | 1, 2.5, 5, 8, 12, 16 oz. |
| Artic / Distilled Water | Ephrata Diamond Spring Water Co. | 1 |
| Artic / Spring Water | Ephrata Diamond Spring Water Co. | 1 |
| Best Yet / Spring Water | Ephrata Diamond Spring Water Co. | 1 |
| Big K / Artesian Water | Deep Rock Water Company | 1, 2, .5 |
| Big K / Distilled Water | Deep Rock Water Company | 1, 5 |
| Carolina Mountain Water / Drinking Water | Carolina Mountain Spring Water Company | 1, 3, 5 |
| Cloister / Distilled Water | Cloister Pure Spring Water Co. | 1, 5 |
| Cloister / Spring Water | Cloister Pure Spring Water Co. | .5, 1, 5, 0.4, 1.1, 1 qt. |
| Crystal Rock / Premium Drinking Water | Crystal Rock Spring Water Co. | .5, 2.5, 5 |
| Crystal / Crystal Fresh Water | McKesson Water Products Company | 1, 2.5, 3, 5 |
| Crystal / Fresh Water with Fluoride | McKesson Water Products Company | 5 |
| Crystal / Mountain Spring Water | McKesson Water Products Company | 5 |

*All sizes measured in gallons unless indicated otherwise

# TABLE 15, CONTINUED

| TRADE NAME/PRODUCT TYPE | MANUFACTURER | SIZE* |
|---|---|---|
| Crystal / Purified Water | McKesson Water Products Company | 1, 5 |
| Culligan / Purified Water | Culligan International Company | 5 |
| Culligan / Sodium Free Drinking Water | Culligan International Company | 5 |
| Deep Rock / Distilled Water | Deep Rock Water Company | .5, 1, 2, 5 |
| Deep Rock / Drinking Water | Deep Rock Water Company | 1, 2.5, 5 |
| Deep Rock / Natural Artesian Water | Deep Rock Water Company | .5, 1, 2, 5 |
| Diamond Water / Distilled Water | Diamond Water, Inc. | 1, 5 |
| Diamond Water / Spring Water | Diamond Water, Inc. | 1, 5 |
| Eau Naturalle / Distilled Water | Ephrata Diamond Spring Water Co. | 5 |
| Endless Mountain / Distilled Water | Ephrata Diamond Spring Water Co. | 5 |
| Ephrata Diamond Spring / Drinking Water | Ephrata Diamond Spring Water Co. | 1, 5 |
| Ephrata Diamond Spring / Spring Water | Ephrata Diamond Spring Water Co. | .5, 1, 5 |
| Eureka / Distilled Water | Eureka Water Company | 1 |
| Eureka / Drinking Water | Eureka Water Company | 1; 10 L |
| Evian / Natural Spring Water | S.A. Des Eaux Minerales D'Evian | .25, .33, .5, 1, 1.5 L |
| Fountainhead / Natural Artesian Water | Fountainhead Water Company | 5, 1, 1.5 L, 5, 12 oz. |
| Georgia Mountain Water / Distilled Water | Georgia Mountain Water, Inc. | 1, 3, 5 |
| Georgia Mountain Water / Spring Water | Georgia Mountain Water, Inc. | 1, 3, 5 |
| Great American / Spring Water | AquaPenn Spring Water Company | 1, 1.5 L, 12, 16 oz. |
| Great Glacier / Artesian | Neenah Springs, Inc. | 1, 2.5 |
| Hinckley & Schmidt / Artesian Water | Hinckley & Schmidt, Inc. | 2.5, 5, 136 oz. |

| | | |
|---|---|---|
| Hinckley & Schmidt / Distilled Water | Hinckley & Schmidt, Inc. | 1, 5, 6, 10 L, 8, 136 oz. |
| Hinckley & Schmidt / Drinking Water | Hinckley & Schmidt, Inc. | 1, 3, 5, 10 L, 8, 136 oz. |
| Hinckley & Schmidt / Mountain Spring Water | Hinckley & Schmidt, Inc. | 1 , 10 L, 8 oz. |
| Hinckley & Schmidt / Natural Spring Water | Hinckley & Schmidt, Inc. | 1, 5, 10 L, 136 oz. |
| Hinckley & Schmidt / Nursery Water | Hinckley & Schmidt, Inc. | 136 oz. |
| Hoosier / Natural Drinking Water | Hinckley & Schmidt, Inc. | 1, 2.5, 5 |
| Hoosier / Pure Steam Distilled Water | Hinckley & Schmidt, Inc. | 1, 2.5, 5 |
| Klarbrunn Sparkling Water | Klarbrunn, Inc. | 12, 16 oz. |
| Leisure Time / Spring Water | Leisure Time Spring Water | .5, 1, 2.5, 3, 5, 6; 1, 1.5 L 12, 16 oz.; 1 pt. |
| Magnetic Springs / Artesian Water | Magnetic Springs Water Company | 1, 2.5, 5 |
| Magnetic Springs / Distilled Water | Magnetic Springs Water Company | 1, 2.5, 5 |
| Magnetic Springs / Drinking Water | Magnetic Springs Water Company | 1, 2.5, 3, 5 |
| Magnetic Springs / Infants Choice | Magnetic Springs Water Company | 1 |
| Midas / Distilled Water | Triton Water Company | 1, 2.5 |
| Midas / Spring Water | Triton Water Company | 1 |
| Minnehaha / Spring Water | Minnehaha Spring Water Co. | 1, 2.5, 5; 1.5 L |
| Minnehaha / Star-Tech Distilled | Minnehaha Spring Water Co. | 1, 5 |
| Mississippi Bottled Water / Distilled Water | Mississippi Bottled Water Company | 1, 5 |
| Mississippi Bottled Water / Drinking Water | Mississippi Bottled Water Company | 1, 5 |
| Mississippi Bottled Water / Fluoridated Water | Mississippi Bottled Water Company | 5 |

*All sizes measured in gallons unless indicated otherwise

**T A B L E   1 5 ,   C O N T I N U E D**

| TRADE NAME/PRODUCT TYPE | MANUFACTURER | SIZE* |
|---|---|---|
| Mississippi Bottled Water / Spring Water | Mississippi Bottled Water Company | 1, 5 |
| Mount Olympus / Distilled Water | Mount Olympus Waters, Inc. | 1, 2.5, 5 |
| Mount Olympus / Purified | Mount Olympus Waters, Inc. | 1 |
| Mount Olympus / Spring Water | Mount Olympus Waters, Inc. | 1, 2.5, 5 |
| Mountain Valley / Spring Water | Mountain Valley Spring Co. | 5, .5, 1, 1.5 L, 10, 12, 16, 64 oz. |
| Natural Water | Keystone / Ozone Pure Water Co. | 5 |
| Neenah Springs / Artesian | Neenah Springs, Inc. | 1, 2.5, 3, 5, 6 |
| Neenah Springs / Distilled | Neenah Springs, Inc. | 1, 2.5, 3, 5, 6 |
| Ozarka / Distilled Water | Eureka Water Company | 1 |
| Ozarka / Drinking Water | Eureka Water Company | 1, 5 ; 10 L |
| Ozarka / Spring Water | Eureka Water Company | 1, 5 ; 10 L |
| Pocono Springs / Pure Mountain Spring Water | Pocono Springs Co. | 1, 2.5, 3, 5, 6; 1, 1.5 L; 16 oz. |
| Publix / Deionized Water | Publix Super Markets, Inc. | 1 |
| Publix / Drinking Water | Publix Super Markets, Inc. | 1, 2.5 |
| Publix / Purified Water | Publix Super Markets, Inc. | 1 |
| Pure American / Spring Water | AquaPenn Spring Water Company | 1, 1.5 L, 12, 16 oz. |
| Puro / Drinking Water | Puro Corporation of America | 5 |
| Puro / Spring Water | Puro Corporation of America | 5 |
| Redners / Spring Water | Ephrata Diamond Spring Water Co. | 1 |
| Roaring Spring / Distilled Water | Roaring Spring Bottling | 1, 5 |
| Roaring Spring / Premium Spring Water | Roaring Spring Bottling | 1, 2.5, 3, 5, 16 oz. |

| Product | Company | Sizes |
|---|---|---|
| Shamrock / Distilled Water | Eureka Water Company | 1, 5 ; 10 L |
| SKH / Spring Water | Ephrata Diamond Spring Water Co. | 1 |
| Snow Valley / Spring Water | Snow Valley, Inc. | 1, 2.5, 5; 1, 1.5 L; 10, 16 oz. |
| Sparkletts / Crystal Fluoridated Drinking Water | McKesson Water Products Company | 3, 5 |
| Sparkletts / Crystal Fluoridated Water | McKesson Water Products Company | 3, 5 |
| Sparkletts / Crystal Fresh Drinking Water | McKesson Water Products Company | 1, 2.5, 5 |
| Sparkletts / Crystal Fresh Water | McKesson Water Products Company | 3, 5 |
| Sparkletts / Distilled Water | McKesson Water Products Company | 1, 2.5 |
| Sparkletts / Drinking Water | McKesson Water Products Company | 1, 2.5, 3, 5 |
| Sparkletts / Purified Water | McKesson Water Products Company | 1, 3, 5 |
| Sparkletts / Spring Water | McKesson Water Products Company | 1, 2.5, 3, 5 |
| Thorofare / Distilled Water | Ephrata Diamond Spring Water Co. | 1 |
| Thorofare / Spring Water | Ephrata Diamond Spring Water Co. | 1 |
| Triple Springs / Natural Spring Water | Triple Springs Spring Water Co. | 3, 5 |
| Triton / Distilled Water | Triton Water Company | .5, 1, 2.5, 6, .5 pt. |
| Triton / Spring Water | Triton Water Company | .5, 1, 2, .5, 1 pt. |
| Wissahickon / Distilled Water | Wissahickon Spring Water, Inc. | 1, 5 |
| Wissahickon / Spring Water | Wissahickon Spring Water, Inc. | 1, 5; 16 oz. |

*All sizes measured in gallons unless indicated otherwise

Source: NSF-International

# 7

# Change the World

It is a sobering commentary that despite all the marvels of this modern technological age, the majority of Americans drinking water from the kitchen faucet incur some level of health risk on a daily basis. We can assure ourselves of a reliably safe drinking water supply in the short run only by purifying our water at home or by purchasing treated water at a premium price. We can change that, however, by convincing our elected representatives that having clean, safe drinking water is a high-priority issue for us. The technology to accomplish this is not expensive and is probably less costly than the amount we spend each year on bottled water and home purification, which at last count totaled $3.5 billion.

If we add in the costs associated with drinking unsafe water, money spent providing all Americans with clean water can truly be seen as an investment, rather than a cost. Consider that the 1993 *Cryptosporidium* outbreak in Milwaukee was estimated to have cost more than $100 million in lost wages, medical costs, and other amounts spent to deal with the crisis. Multiply that amount across the board to include sicknesses, cancer deaths, lead-induced learning impairments, and other ailments caused by contaminated drinking water throughout the nation and the value of investing in water treatment facilities becomes even more obvious.

The legislative steps needed to improve our drinking water supply are well known. The problem is not insufficient information or inadequate technology. We know the answers. The only missing piece to the clean drinking water puzzle is political will. As voters and taxpayers, we must *demand* that our elected representatives at every level of government become committed to assuring a safe drinking water supply to all Americans. Some of the recommended steps for improving the Safe Drinking Water Act and the Clean Water Act are outlined below. Following that section is information about how to write to your elected representatives and a list of organizations already involved in the fight for clean drinking water.

## SPECIFIC STEPS TO IMPROVE OUR DRINKING WATER

**1. More protection at the source.** Protecting watersheds and groundwater from chemical and animal wastes, and from erosion due to development, helps to ensure a cleaner drinking water supply for years to come. The Clean Water Act, the Safe Drinking Water Act, and Farm Bill legislation should be strengthened to reduce the amount of urban runoff, sewage overflow, and industrial and farm waste that flow into rivers, lakes, and aquifers—the sources of our drinking water.

**2. Ensure basic treatment for all water systems.** With the exception of systems with pure source water, all large systems must have the basic technologies—sedimentation, coagulation, and/or filtration—to treat drinking water.

**3. Modern technology for systems that need it.** Cities and towns with water supplies contaminated by industrial waste or pesticide runoff must install either granular activated carbon filtration or other advanced purification systems. Currently, less than 10 percent of large systems use these modern techniques. At an estimated $30 per year per household, or less, cost simply should not be a barrier. For poor or small communities, revolving state loan funds and federal grants can pick up some of the slack, and higher fines for polluters can help as well. Finally, consolidating many small systems will enable them to operate more efficiently and to afford better testing, monitoring, and purification.

**4. Improvement of distribution systems.** Crumbling water mains, lead and lead-coated service lines, and leaking waste and sewage lines must be upgraded, improved, or replaced. As with source protection and purification improvements, these measures can be paid for over time and will ultimately save far more than they cost.

**5. Improvements to the Clean Water Act and Safe Drinking Water Act.** New or strengthened provisions must include:

- Enforcing strict environmental protection for watersheds within surface water–supplied drinking water systems and for areas that drain into aquifers used for drinking water.

- Providing financial assistance to needy local public water districts from a revolving loan fund.

- Charging a federal user's fee of about 10 cents per 1,000 gallons of water, to be used to fund drinking water cleanup in states that refuse to take action on their own or do not fully fund their own programs.

- Providing technical assistance to small systems, including assistance in their consolidation.

- Strengthening public notification requirements and requirements of public access to information about drinking water contamination.

- Banning all lead in plumbing, faucets, fixtures, and other components that come in contact with drinking water. Current law allows fixtures to be sold as "lead free" if they contain less than 10 percent lead, which is still enough to contaminate water.

- Increasing the budget for enforcement, state grants, research, and other Safe Drinking Water Act provisions that will help provide all Americans with healthy, safe water from the faucets in our homes.

- Strengthening enforcement by the Environmental

Protection Agency and state authorities, including higher penalties for non-compliance, and strengthening citizen-suit provision within the Safe Drinking Water Act.

- Providing funding supplements to aid systems in improving their source protection, treatment, and distribution systems. The $4.6 billion state revolving loan fund proposed by the Clinton administration in 1994 was an example of the possibilities that would enable water systems to finance the upgrading of their facilities.

## Unfunded Mandates

The opponents of strong drinking water protection complain that when the federal government forces states or local governments to protect the environment without providing money to pay for it, this amounts to an "unfunded mandate" and is unfair. As Carl Pope, executive director of the Sierra Club and an observer of the unfunded mandate argument, noted in 1994, "The logic of unfunded mandates would have the federal government paying for pasteurizing milk, keeping chickens free of salmonella, and footing the bill for meeting virtually any health standard it sets."

Keep in mind that 88 percent of the members of Congress who voted to weaken water standards in 1994 have bottled water delivered to their Capitol Hill offices, water paid for by taxpayers. What's good enough for Congress is good enough for all Americans; we must *demand* improvements to the Safe Drinking Water Act.

The unfunded mandate crowd proposes to save money by letting the poor, the elderly, the chronically ill, and school children drink unsafe water, while those who can afford it turn to bottled water or home purification. Inadequate drinking water laws make safe drinking water a privilege available only to some Americans. We can make it the right of all.

Demand of your senator, congressperson, governor, mayor or county commissioners, and public water agencies that they strengthen, not weaken, the Safe Drinking Water Act.

## Who to Write

Use the following addresses to send letters demanding some or all of the measures listed above. Personally written letters get more attention than pre-packaged postcards or computer-printed letters, but all letters help convince elected officials to respond to voters' concerns.

### The President
*President Clinton (or his successor)*
*The White House*
*1600 Pennsylvania Avenue, NW*
*Washington, DC 20500*

### Your Mayor, Governor, Congressperson, and Two Senators

The phone number for Voter Registration can be found in the Government section of your phone book. The Voter Registration office can provide you with the names and addresses of your mayor, governor, congressperson, and two senators. Send letters to all of them demanding clean water and listing some of the recommendations outlined above. Demand stronger environmental protection laws in general. Demand laws that make polluters pay, which increases the cost of polluting to those who foul our water to begin with.

Together, our voices will be heard.

### Organizations Working to Protect Your Drinking Water

The following organizations are fighting to protect the environment from pollution and to strengthen drinking water protections. They can provide you with up-to-date information about these issues, and by supporting them you can add impact to their efforts.

Sierra Club
730 Polk Street
San Francisco, CA 94109
(415) 776-2211

Natural Resources Defense
  Council
40 West 20th Street
New York, NY 10011
(212) 727-2700

Friends of the Earth
218 D St., SE
Washington, DC 20003
(202) 783-7400

Greenpeace
1436 U St., NW
Washington, DC 20009
(202) 462-1177

Environmental Defense Fund
1875 Connecticut Ave., NW
Suite 1016
Washington, DC 20009
(202) 387-3500

Environmental Working
  Group
1718 Connecticut Ave. NW
Suite 600
Washington, DC 20009
(202) 667-6982

## Vote Green

Voting is the most direct means of influencing the political process. Examine the environmental voting records of each candidate. Make environmental issues a primary criterion for choosing a candidate. To monitor voting records, contact: The League of Conservation Voters, 1150 Connecticut Avenue, NW, Washington, DC 20036, (202) 785-8683. You can also call the Sierra Club in Washington, D.C., for more information at (202) 547-1141.

## Be an Environmentalist

Reduce your consumption of disposable products; yard, garden, and home pesticides; and cleaners made with toxic chemicals. Recycle. Be a green consumer. Buy organic produce if you can; it's sometimes more expensive, but healthier for you and the planet, and as more people buy organic, prices will continue to decline.

Teach your children, parents, and friends the importance of practicing environmental awareness in day-to-day life. Share with them what you have learned about drinking water issues. Start a discussion group, or an action group, at your community center, religious organization, or social club.

Every effort counts!

# Water of Life

**F**amiliar images of the earth show a beautiful blue sphere, fringed with white, hanging against the black vastness of space. The seas, the clouds, and the ice caps—viewed from afar, these are the predominant features of our watery globe. Indeed, the circulation of water drives the climate, the land-based and marine ecosystems, and the life of every plant and animal on earth. Water carries nutrients from mountain top to valley floor and on to the sea, and through the cells of every living being along the way. No matter how we try, the biological and chemical effluvia of the human project do not escape us for long; water returns them to us with the certainty of the tides. In this is water's great lesson.

For millennia, humanity lived in a tenuous balance with the natural cycles that sustained its survival. The advent of industrialization and rapid population growth have since shifted that balance, and as we lurch precariously toward the edge of irreversible ecological harm, a whisper has begun to spread through communities and nations. The present course is not working, it says. Despite the seductions of material comfort, and the promise of insulation from the desperate conditions of the majority of humankind, we have a nagging sense of something wrong, which echoes like a bell in the distance. We live in the generation of decision.

The warning signs of a crisis surround us—vanishing species, accumulating toxins at every level of the food chain, the unraveling ozone layer. If the warnings don't impact us directly and immediately, we too often slip into the easy rhythm of apathy or hopelessness, but only at our peril.

There is ample reason for hope, with abundant opportunities for each of us to become an activist for environmental change. The anti-environmental forces are strong: They are funded by multi-billion-dollar corporations that profit from destroying, and are supported by individuals either unwilling to take an honest look at the state of the planet or uncaring enough to insist that the ways of the past are adequate to face the problems of the future. Nevertheless, significant strides have been made in stopping pollution at the source and tightening the regulations that protect drinking water supplies. We must be vigilant in our commitment to see the environmental laws strengthened, and to make sure those stronger laws get enforced.

Nothing is more fundamental to our life than the water we drink. Over two-thirds of our body mass consists of nothing else. The water pouring from our taps may carry the toxins of the world we live in, bringing home to us the poisons sprayed on our food crops or used in our factories. For the present, to protect our health, our task is to reduce these contaminants before we drink the water. This book is a tool for that purpose.

For the future, our goal must be to keep these contaminants from the water to begin with. More than our health is at stake. The pollution that fouls our drinking water is poisoning wildlife, ravaging entire ecosystems, and burning a hole in the fragile fabric of life itself.

One strategy of the anti-environmentalists is to give environmentalism a bad name. Don't let them. Declare your allegiance to the rivers, lakes, and streams, to the wild lands and wildlife that still remain. State to yourself, and to the world, your commitment to protecting your health and that of your neighbors, your children, your great-great-grandchildren to come.

Those who benefit in the short run from the production, use, or sale of polluting substances and those in government who oppose environmental protection as a matter of principle or self-interest must be met with firm, resolute opposition.

Someday, perhaps before the time of our great-great-grandchildren, someone will turn on the faucet to take a drink of water. It is possible that coming from that tap will be water clean, pure, and healthy, free from the contaminants of a polluting society. We can make that happen.

# AFTERWORD

**W**ater, a strange unity between hydrogen and oxygen, is essential for all life on earth. Water is the key ingredient of mother's milk and snake venom, honey and tears. Though our earth is awash in it, water is no one single thing. It is a contradiction, a riddle. As the Chinese say, water can both sink and float a boat.

Our bodies are mostly water; our blood mimics the same delicate balance of salt and minerals as the sea. Although we are not always conscious of the profound connection between our physical selves and the mystery of water, we nevertheless choose to call great pools of the liquid "bodies of water."

History shows that without a steady supply of clean, safe water, ancient civilizations have vanished. For our own historical touchstone, twenty-seven years lends perspective enough. In June 1969 Ohio's Cuyahoga River, laden with toxic wastes, burst into flames. That symbolized all that had gone wrong with America's waters, and we demanded action. Congress responded.

The Clean Water Act and its public-policy twin, the Safe Drinking Water Act, were visionary pacts between the people and their federal government. In writing these laws, our representatives in Washington promised clean, safe water to all Americans. The Clean Water Act's stated goals were to make the nation's waters "drinkable, fishable, swimmable." The Safe Drinking Water Act's goals were even more clear: water for health.

Since these landmark laws passed, we have made progress by anyone's standards. For instance, pollution control has reduced releases of toxins into our waters by more than 1 billion pounds each year. Not only that, but the percentage of Americans served by effective sewage treatment grew from

42 to 58 percent between 1970 and 1988, at the same time that the population ballooned.

Scott Lewis acknowledges the strides we have made in protecting our nation's waters but the promises of the landmark laws are still largely unfulfilled. Many contaminants in our drinking water go unregulated, and for those chemicals that are under regulation, enforcement can be lax. From 1992 to 1994, more than 35 million people drank water from water systems that violated EPA drinking water standards. Another 80 million people drank water from systems that violated reporting rules. In 1993, the city of Milwaukee suffered the largest waterborne-disease outbreak in modern U.S. history, killing more than 100 of its residents. A year later, the city of Las Vegas suffered a similar fate, with seven fatalities. Clearly, there's still trouble on tap.

Lewis knows that it was public opinion that drove passage of the Clean Water Act and the Safe Drinking Water Act. He wrote this book knowing that in every opinion poll Americans single out clean, safe water as their top environmental concern. This support cuts across political and economic lines, and is consistent year after year.

But there's a gap between the polls and the pols on issues of clean water. Blind to the public interest, bound to the interest groups, the 103rd Congress proposed—but did not approve—a law that would roll back protection of our water. The law would have meant more toxins in our streams and lakes, more poisons in our drinking wells. Already, the 104th Congress, a more hostile and active bunch, has underway a bill that is even more frightening. Why?

Perhaps the members of the 104th Congress have become so totally disconnected from the rules of nature that they can easily rationalize making their own rules, rules that would allow for the destruction of nature. After all, they can insulate themselves. A Sierra Club survey recently found that 88 percent of the members of Congress who voted to weaken water standards in 1994 had bottled water delivered to their Capitol

Hill offices—at the taxpayers' expense. At our expense. So before we buy our senators another drink, let's find out what's on tap.

Armed with the information Scott Lewis has so painstakingly assembled here, we will go once again to the policy makers. We will demand that they deliver on the promise of clean, safe water for all Americans. They will eventually respond, not because we have information, and not even because that information is true and compelling. They will respond because we will insist.

Carl Pope

Executive Director, Sierra Club

# Suggested Reading

### Drinking Water

Cameron, Diane, Brett Hulsey, and John Peck. "Danger on Tap: Protect America's Drinking Water." Madison, Wisconsin: Sierra Club Great Lakes Program, 1994.

Cohen, Brian, Christopher Campbell, and Richard Wiles. "In the Drink." Washington, D.C.: Environmental Working Group, 1995. Available on the World Wide Web at: <http://www.ewg.org>

Cohen, Brian, Richard Wiles, and Edmund Bondoc. "Weed Killers by the Glass: A Citizens' Tap Water Monitoring Project in 29 Cities." Washington, D.C.: Environmental Working Group, 1995. Available on the World Wide Web at: <http://www.ewg.org>

Olson, Erik. "You Are What You Drink...*Cryptosporidium* and Other Contaminants Found in the Water Served to Millions of Americans." Washington, D.C.: Natural Resources Defense Council, 1995.

Olson, Erik, and Brian Cohen. "Victorian Water Treatment Enters the 21st Century." Washington, D.C.: Natural Resources Defense Council, 1994.

Olson, Erik. "Think Before You Drink, the Failure of the Nation's Drinking Water System." Washington, D.C., Natural Resources Defense Council, 1993.

### Related Subjects

*Some helpful resources for learning how we can keep pollution from the environment in the first place:*

Dadd, Debra Lynn. "Nontoxic, Natural, and Earthwise: How

to Protect Yourself and Your Family from Harmful Products and Live in Harmony with the Earth." New York: Putnam Publishing, 1993.

Hunter, Linda Mason. *The Healthy Home, an Attic-to-Basement Guide to Toxin-Free Living*. Emmaus, Pennsylvania: Rodale Press, 1989.

Schultz, Warren. *The Chemical-Free Lawn*. Emmaus, Pennsylvania: Rodale Press, 1989.

Schoemaker, Joyce, and Charity Vitale. *Healthy Homes, Healthy Kids: Protecting Your Children from Everyday Environmental Hazards*. Washington, D.C.: Island Press, 1991.

*A visionary workplan for a realistic, sustainable economy:*

Hawkin, Paul., *The Ecology of Commerce: A Declaration of Sustainability*. New York: HarperCollins, 1993.

# APPENDIX A

# EPA Drinking Water Standards

The Safe Drinking Water Act requires the EPA to issue maximum contaminant level standards for substances known to be harmful to human health and known to pollute drinking water. These are the national Primary Drinking Water Standards. In cases where it is not technologically or economically feasible to determine how much of a contaminant is present in drinking water, the EPA can set treatment technique standards instead—specific treatment methods to be used to control that contaminant.

Unlike the Primary Standards, which are designed to protect public health, Secondary Drinking Water Standards are designed to protect "public welfare" by providing guidelines regarding the taste, odor, color, and other aesthetic aspects of drinking water. However, some substances on the Secondary Standards list, such as aluminium, have been identified as probable health risks, but have not yet been elevated to primary status. Also, many substances known to be a health risk, such as the microorganism *Cryptosporidium* and dozens of synthetic chemicals, are not subject to any standards at all.

Table 16 presents the national Primary Drinking Water Standards for thirty contaminants. In addition to MCLs, the health effects and sources of each contaminant are listed. Table 17 presents the Secondary Drinking Water Standards.

## T A B L E  1 6

## National Primary Drinking Water Standards

| CONTAMINANTS | MCL (mg/L) | POTENTIAL HEALTH EFFECTS | SOURCES OF CONTAMINATION |
|---|---|---|---|
| **Coliform and Surface Water Treatment** | | | |
| *Giardia lamblia* | TT | Giardiasis | Human and animal fecal waste |
| *Legionella* | TT | Legionnaire's disease | Indigenous to natural waters; can grow in water heating systems |
| Standard Plate Count | TT | Indicates water quality, effectiveness of treatment | |
| Total Coliform | <5% | Indicates gastroenteric pathogens | Human and animal fecal waste |
| Turbidity | TT | Interferes with disinfection, filtration | Soil runoff |
| Viruses | TT | Gastroenteric disease | Human and animal fecal waste |
| **Inorganics** | | | |
| Antimony | | Cancer | Fire retardants, ceramics, electronics, fireworks, solder |
| Asbestos | | Cancer | Natural deposits; asbestos cement in water systems |
| Barium | | Kidney effects | Natural deposits; pigments, epoxy sealants, spent coal |
| Beryllium | | Bone, lung damage | Electrical, aerospace, defense industries |
| Cadmium | | Kidney effects | Galvanized pipe corrosion; natural deposits; batteries, paints |
| Chromium | | Liver, kidney, circulatory disorders | Natural deposits; mining, electroplating, pigments |

# TABLE 16, CONTINUED

| CONTAMINANTS | MCL (mg/L) | POTENTIAL HEALTH EFFECTS | SOURCES OF CONTAMINATION |
|---|---|---|---|
| **Inorganics, continued** | | | |
| Copper | | Gastrointestinal irritation | Natural/industrial deposits; wood preservatives, plumbing |
| Cyanide | | Thyroid, nervous system damage | Electroplating, steel, plastics, mining, fertilizer |
| Fluoride | | Skeletal and dental fluorosis | Natural deposits; fertilizer, aluminum industries; water additive |
| Lead | | Kidney, nervous system damage | Natural/industrial deposits; plumbing, solder, brass alloy faucets |
| Nickel | | Heart, liver damage | Metal alloys, electroplating, batteries, chemical production |
| Nitrate | | Methemoglobulinemia (Blue Baby Syndrome) | Animal waste, fertilizer, natural deposits, septic tanks, sewage |
| Nitrite | | Methemoglobulinemia (Blue Baby Syndrome) | Same as nitrate; rapidly converts to nitrate |
| Selenium | | Liver damage | Natural deposits; mining, smelting, coal/oil combustion |
| Thallium | | Kidney, liver, brain, intestinal | Electronics, drugs, alloys, glass |
| **Organics and Volatile Organics** | | | |
| Acrylamide | TT | Cancer, nervous system effects | Polymers used in sewage/wastewater treatment |
| Alachlor | 0.002 | Cancer | Runoff from herbicide on corn, soybeans, other crops |
| Adipate, (di(2-ethylhexyl)) | 0.4 | Decreased body weight; liver and testes damage | Synthetic rubber, food packaging, cosmetics |

## TABLE 16, CONTINUED

### Organics and Volatile Organics, continued

| CONTAMINANTS | MCL (mg/L) | POTENTIAL HEALTH EFFECTS | SOURCES OF CONTAMINATION |
|---|---|---|---|
| Aldicarb | 0.003 | Nervous system effects | Insecticide on cotton, potatoes, others |
| Aldicarb sulfone | 0.002 | Nervous system effects | Biodegradation of aldicarb |
| Aldicarb sulfoxide | 0.004 | Nervous system effects | Biodegradation of aldicarb |
| Atrazine | 0.003 | Breast cancer | Runoff from use as herbicide on corn and non-cropland |
| Benzene | 0.005 | Cancer | Some foods; gas, drugs, pesticide, paint, plastics industries |
| Carbofuran | 0.04 | Nervous, reproductive system effects | Soil fumigant on corn and cotton |
| Carbon tetrachloride | 0.005 | Cancer | Solvents and their degradation products |
| Chlordane | 0.002 | Cancer | Leaching from soil treatment for termites |
| Chlorobenzene | 0.1 | Nervous system and liver effects | Waste solvent from metal degreasing processes |
| Dalapon | 0.2 | Liver, kidney | Herbicide on orchards, beans, coffee, lawns, road, roadways |
| Dichloromethane | 0.005 | Cancer | Paint stripper; metal degreaser; propellant; extraction |
| 2,4,-D | 0.07 | Liver and kidney damage | Runoff from herbicide on wheat, corn, rangelands, lawns |
| o-Dichlorobenzene | 0.6 | Liver, kidney, and blood cell damage | Paints; engine cleaning compounds; dyes; chemical wastes |
| p-Dichlorobenzene | 0.075 | Cancer | Room and water deodorants, and "mothballs" |

## TABLE 16, CONTINUED

### Organics and Volatile Organics, continued

| CONTAMINANTS | MCL (mg/L) | POTENTIAL HEALTH EFFECTS | SOURCES OF CONTAMINATION |
|---|---|---|---|
| 1,2-Dichloroethane | 0.005 | Cancer | Leaded gas, fumigants, paints |
| 1,1-Dichloroethane | 0.007 | Cancer | Plastics, dyes, perfumes, paints |
| cis-1,2-Dichloroethylene | 0.07 | Liver, kidney, nervous and circulatory systems | Waste industrial extraction solvents |
| trans-1,2-Dichloroethylene | 0.1 | Liver, kidney, nervous and circulatory systems | Waste industrial extraction solvents |
| Dibromochloropropane | 0.0002 | Cancer | Soil fumigant on soybeans, cotton, pineapple, orchards |
| 1,2-Dichloropropane | 0.005 | Liver, kidney effects; cancer | Soil fumigant; waste industrial solvents |
| Dinoseb | 0.007 | Thyroid, reproductive organ damage | Runoff of herbicide from crop and non-crop applications |
| Dioxin | 0.000000003 | Cancer | Chemical production by-product; impurity in herbicides |
| Diquat | 0.02 | Liver, kidney, eye effects | Runoff of herbicide on land and aquatic weeds |
| Endothall | 0.1 | Liver, kidney, gastrointestinal | Herbicide on crops, weeds |
| Epichlorohydrin | TT | Cancer | Water treatment chemicals; waste epoxy resins, coatings |
| Ethylbenzene | 0.7 | Liver, kidney, nervous system | Gasoline; insecticides; chemical manufacturing wastes |
| Ethylene dibromide | 0.00005 | Cancer | Leaded gas additives; leaching of soil fumigant |
| Glyphosate | 0.7 | Liver, kidney damage | Herbicide on grasses, weeds, brush |
| Heptachlor | 0.0004 | Cancer | Leaching of insecticide for termites |

**TABLE 16, CONTINUED**

## Organics and Volatile Organics, continued

| CONTAMINANTS | MCL (mg/L) | POTENTIAL HEALTH EFFECTS | SOURCES OF CONTAMINATION |
|---|---|---|---|
| Heptachlor epoxide | 0.0002 | Cancer | Biodegradation of heptachlor |
| Hexachlorobenzene | 0.001 | Cancer | Pesticide production waste by-product |
| Hexachlorocyclopentadiene | 0.05 | Kidney, stomach damage | Pesticide production, intermediate step |
| Oxamyl (Vydate) | 0.2 | Kidney damage | Insecticide on apples, potatoes, tomatoes |
| PAHs(benzo(a)pyrene) | 0.0002 | Cancer | Coal tar coatings; burning organic matter, volcanoes, fossil fuels |
| Phthalate,(di(2-ethylhexyl)) | 0.006 | Cancer | PVC and other plastics |
| Picloram | 0.6 | Kidney, liver damage | Herbicide on broadleaf and woody plants |
| Simazine | 0.006 | Cancer | Herbicide on grass sod, some crops, aquatic algae |
| 1,2,4-Trichlorobenzene | 0.07 | Liver, kidney damage | Herbicide production; dye carrier |
| Trichloroethylene | 0.005 | Cancer, liver and kidney effects | Textiles, adhesives and metal degreasers |
| 1,1,1-Trichloroethylene | 0.2 | Liver, nervous system effects | Adhesives, aerosols, textiles, paints, inks, metal degreasers |
| 1,1,2-Trichloroethane | 0.005 | Kidney, liver, nervous system | Solvent in rubber, other organic poducts; chemcial production wastes |
| Vinyl chloride | 0.002 | Cancer | May leach from PVC pipe; formed by solvent breakdown |

## TABLE 16, CONTINUED

| CONTAMINANTS | MCL (mg/L) | POTENTIAL HEALTH EFFECTS | SOURCES OF CONTAMINATION |
|---|---|---|---|
| **Other Proposed (P) and Interim (I) Standards** | | | |
| Beta/photon emitters (I) and (P) | 4 mrem/yr | Cancer | Decay of radionuclides in natural and human-made deposits |
| Alpha emitters (I) and (P) | 15 pCi/L | Cancer | Decay of radionuclides in natural deposits |
| Combined Radium 226/228 | 5 pCi/L | Bone Cancer | Natural deposits |
| Radium 226 (P) | 20 pCi/L | Bone Cancer | Natural deposits |
| Radium 228 (P) | 20 pCi/L | Bone Cancer | Natural deposits |
| Radon (P) | 300 pCi/L | Cancer | Decay of radionuclides in natural deposits |
| Uranium (P) | 0.02 | Cancer | Natural deposits |
| Sulfate (P) | 400/500 | Diarrhea | Natural deposits |
| Arsenic (I) | 0.05 | Skin, nervous system | Natural deposits |
| Total trihalomethanes (I) | 0.10 | Cancer | Drinking water chlorination by-products |

pCi = picocurie—a measure of radioactivity

mrem = millirems, a measure of radiation absorbed by the body

TT = Treatment technique requirement

MFL = Million fibers per Liter

TABLE 17

# Secondary Drinking Water Standards

| CONTAMINANTS | SUGGESTED LEVELS | CONTAMINANT EFFECTS |
| --- | --- | --- |
| Aluminum | 0.05-0.2 mg/L | Discoloration of water |
| Chloride | 250 mg/L | Salty taste; corrosion of pipes |
| Color | 15 color units | Visible tint |
| Copper | 1.0 mg/L | Metallic taste; blue/green staining of porcelain |
| Corrosivity | non-corrosive | Metallic taste; fixture staining, corroded pipes (Corrosive water can leach pipe materials, such as lead, into drinking water) |
| Fluoride | 2.0 mg/L | Dental fluorosis (a brownish discoloration of the teeth) |
| Foaming agents | 0.5 mg/L | Aesthetic—Frothy, cloudy, bitter taste, odor |
| Iron | 0.3 mg/L | Bitter metallic taste; staining of laundry, rusty color, sediment |
| Mangangese | 0.05 mg/L | Taste; staining of laundry, black-to-brown color, black staining |
| Odor | 3 threshold odor | "Rotten egg," musty, or chemical smell |
| pH | | Low pH—Bitter metallic taste |
| Silver | 0.1 mg/L | Argyria (discoloration of the skin), graying of the eyes |
| Sulfate | 250 mg/L | Salty taste; laxitive effects |
| Total dissolved solids | 500 mg/L | Taste and possible relation between low hardness and cardiovascular disease; indicator of corrosivity (related to lead levels in water); can damage plumbing and limit effectiveness of soaps and detergents |
| Zinc | 5 mg/L | Metallic taste |

# APPENDIX B

# State Water Agencies

## AK

Alaska Drinking Water Program
Wastewater and Water
  Treatment
Environmental Conservation
  Department
410 Willoughby
Juneau, AK 99801
(907) 465-5316

## AL

Water Supply Branch
Dept. of Environmental
  Management
1751 W. L. Dickinson Drive
Montgomery, AL 36130
(205) 271-7773

## AR

Division of Engineering
Arkansas Dept. of Health
Mail Slot 37
4815 West Markham Street
Little Rock, AR 72205-3867
(501) 661-2623

## AZ

Compliance Section
Office of Water Quality
Room 200
3033 North Central
Phoenix, AZ 85001
(602) 207-4617

## CA

Division of Drinking Water
  and Environmental
  Management
CA Department of Health
  Services
714 P Street, Room 692
Sacramento, CA 95814
(916) 323-6111

## CO

Drinking Water Program
WQCD-DW-B2
CO Department of Health
4300 Cherry Creek Drive So.
Denver, CO 80222
(303) 692-3546

## CT

Water Supplies Section
Connecticut Department of
  Health Services
150 Washington Street
Hartford, CT 06106
(203) 566-1253

## DC

Water Hygiene Branch
Department of Consumer and
  Regulatory Affairs
2100 Martin Luther King Ave.
Washington, DC 20020
(202) 404-1120

**DE**
Public Water Systems
   Supervision Program
Division of Public Health
Cooper Building, P.O. Box 637
Federal & Water Streets
Dover, DE 19903
(302) 739-5410

**FL**
Drinking Water Section
Department of Environmental
   Protection
Twin Towers
2600 Blair Stone Road
Tallahassee, FL 32399-2400
(904) 487-1762

**GA**
Drinking Water Program
Environmental Protection
   Division
205 Butler Street SE
Atlanta, GA 30334
(404) 651-5154

**HI**
Environmental Management
   Division
Department of Health
P.O. Box 3378
Honolulu, HI 96801
(808) 586-4304

**IA**
Environmental Protection
   Division
Dept. of Natural Resources
Water Quality Bureau
Wallace State Office Building
900 East Grand Avenue
Des Moines, IA 50319
(515) 281-8869

**ID**
Drinking Water Program
Division of Environmental
   Quality
Department of Health and
   Welfare
1410 North Hilton
Boise, ID 83706
(208) 334-5860

**IL**
Division of Public Water
   Supplies
Illinois EPA
2200 Churchill Road
Springfield, IL 62794-9276
(217) 785-8653

**IN**
Drinking Water Branch
Office of Water Management
IN Dept. of Environmental
   Management
100 North Senate Avenue
Indianapolis, IN 46206-6015
(317) 233-4222

**KS**
Pubic Water Supply Section
Kansas Dept. of Health and
   the Environment
Forbes Field, Building 740
Topeka, KS 66620
(913) 296-5503

**KY**
Division of Water
Drinking Water Branch
Frankfort Office Park
14 Reilly Road
Frankfort, KY 40601
(502) 564-3410

## LA
Office of Public Health
Louisiana Dept. of Health and
  Hospitals
P.O. Box 60630
New Orleans, LA 70160
(504) 568-5105

## MA
Division of Water Supply
Dept. of Environmental
  Protection
One Winter Street
Boston, MA 02108
(617) 292-5529

## MD
Water Supply Program
Maryland Department of
  Environment
2500 Broening Highway
Dunkalk, MD 21224
(410) 631-3702

## ME
Division of Health Engineering
Maine Dept. of Human
  Services
State House (STA 10)
Augusta, ME 04333
(207) 287-2070

## MI
Division of Water Supply
Michigan Department of Public
  Health
P.O. Box 30195
Lansing, MI 48909
(517) 335-8326

## MN
Drinking Water Protection
Minnesota Department of
  Health
925 Delaware St. SE
Minneapolis, MN 55459
(612) 627-5133

## MO
Public Drinking Water Program
Division of Environmental
  Quality
P.O. Box 176
Jefferson City, MO 65102
(314) 751-5331

## MS
Division of Water Supply
MS Department of Health
  Office U-232, P.O. Box 1700
2423 N. State Street
Jackson, MS 39215-1700
(601) 960-7518

## MT
Water Quality Bureau
Department of Health and
  Environmental Sciences
Cogswell Bldg., Room A206
Helena, MT 59620
(406) 444-2406

## NC
Public Water Supply Sec.
Div. of Environmental Health
Dept. of Environment, Health
  and Natural Resources
P.O. Box 27687
Raleigh, NC 27611-7687
(919) 733-2321

**ND**
Division of Water Supply and
  Pollution Control
State Department of Health
1200 Missouri Ave.
Bismarck, ND 58502
(701) 221-5225

**NE**
Division of Drinking Water and
  Environmental Sanitation
NE Department of Health
301 Centennial Mall South
Lincoln, NE 68509
(402) 471-2541 or 0510

**NH**
Water Supply Engineering
  Bureau
Department of Environmental
  Services
6 Hazen Drive
P.O. Box 95
Concord, NH 03302
(603) 271-3503

**NJ**
Bureau of Safe Drinking Water
NJ Dept. of Environmental
  Protection
P.O. Box CN-426
Trenton, NJ 06825
(609) 292-5550

**NM**
Drinking Water Section
New Mexico Health and
  Environment Department
1190 St. Francis Drive
Santa Fe, NM 87503
(505) 827-2778

**NV**
Public Health Engineering
NV Dept. of Human Resources
  Consumer Health
505 East King Street, Room 103
Carson City, NV 89710
(702) 687-6615

**NY**
Bureau of Public Water Supply
  Protection
New York Dept. of Health
2 University Place, Room 406
Albany, NY 12203-3313
(518) 458-6731

**OH**
Division of Ground and
  Drinking Waters
OH Environmental Protection
  Agency
P.O. Box 1049
1800 Watermark Drive
Columbus, OH 43266-1049
(614) 644-2752

**OK**
Water Quality Programs
Dept. of Environmental
  Quality
1000 NE Tenth Street
Oklahoma City, OK 73117
(405) 271-5205

**OR**
Drinking Water Program
  Health Division
Dept. of Human Resources
800 Northeast Oregon Street
Portland, OR 97214-0450
(503) 731-4010

## PA

Division of Drinking Water
Management
Department of Environmental
Resources
P.O. Box 8467
Harrisburg, PA 17107
(717) 787-9035

## RI

Division of Drinking Water
Quality
RI Dept. of Health
75 Davis Street, Cannon Bldg.
Providence, RI 02908
(410) 277-6867

## SC

Bureau of Drinking Water
Protection
Dept. of Health and
Environmental Control
2600 Bull Street
Columbia, SC 29201
(803) 734-5310

## SD

Office of Drinking Water
Department of Water and
Natural Resources
523 Capital Ave./Foss Bldg.
Pierre, SD 57501
(605) 773-3754

## TN

Division of Water Supply
Tennessee Department of
Environment & Conservation
401 Church Street
Nashville, TN 37243-1549
(615) 532-0191

## TX

Water Utilities Division
Natural Resource Conservation
Commission
P.O. Box 13087
Austin, TX 78711
(512) 908-6930

## UT

Division of Drinking Water
UT Department of
Environmental Quality
288 North 1460 West
Salt Lake City, UT 84114
(801) 538-6159

## VA

Division of Water Supply
Engineering
VA Department of Health
1500 East Main Street
Richmond, VA 23219
(804) 786-1766

## VT

Water Supply Program
VT Department of
Environmental Conservation
103 South Main Street
Waterbury, VT 05671
(802) 241-3400

## WA

Drinking Water Division
Department of Health
Airdustrial Center
Building #3
P.O. Box 47822
Olympia, WA 98504-7822
(206) 753-1280

**WI**
Bureau of Water Supply
Department of Natural
  Resources
P.O. Box 7921
Madison, WI 53707
(608) 267-7651

**WV**
Office of Environmental Health
  Services
815 Quarrier Street
Suite 418
Charleston, WV 25301
(304) 558-2981

**WY**
Water Quality Division
Dept. of Environmental
  Quality
Herschler Bldg., 4th Floor
Cheyenne, WY 82002
(307) 777-7781

## Trusts and Territories

**American Samoa**
Environmental Protection
  Agency
Office of the Governor
American Samoa
Pago Pago, American Samoa
  96799
(No number available)

**Guam**
Guam Environmental
  Protection Agency
Government of Guam
130 Rojas Street/Harmon Plaza
Harmon, Guam 96911
(671) 646-8863

**Mariana Islands**
Division of Environmental
  Quality
Commonwealth of the
  Northern Mariana Islands
P.O. Box 1304
Saipan, CM 96950
(670) 234-6114

**Palau**
Palau Environmental Quality
  Protection Board
Republic of Palau
P.O. Box 100
Koror, Palau 96940
(No number available)

**Puerto Rico**
Water Supply Supervision
  Program
Puerto Rico Dept. of Health
P.O. Box 70184
San Juan, PR 00936
(809) 754-6010

**Virgin Islands**
Planning & Natural Resources
Government of Virgin Islands
Nifky Center
Room 231
St. Thomas, VI 00802
(809) 774-3320

# EPA Regional Offices

| *EPA Regional Office* | *States Covered* |
|---|---|
| EPA Region 1<br>JFK Federal Building<br>1 Congress Street<br>Boston, MA 02203 | Connecticut, Maine, Massachusetts,<br>New Hampshire, Rhode Island,<br>Vermont |
| EPA Region 2<br>26 Federal Plaza<br>New York, NY 10278 | New Jersey, New York,<br>Puerto Rico, Virgin Islands |
| EPA Region 3<br>841 Chestnut Street<br>Philadelphia, PA 19107 | Delaware, District of Columbia,<br>Maryland, Pennsylvania,<br>Virginia, West Virginia |
| EPA Region 4<br>345 Courtland St. NE<br>Atlanta, GA 30365 | Alabama, Florida, Georgia,<br>Kentucky, Mississippi, North<br>Carolina, South Carolina, Tennessee |
| EPA Region 5<br>77 West Jackson Blvd.<br>Chicago, IL 60604 | Illinois, Indiana, Michigan,<br>Minnesota, Ohio, Wisconsin |
| EPA Region 6<br>1445 Ross Avenue<br>12th Floor<br>Dallas, TX 75202 | Arkansas, Louisiana, New Mexico,<br>Oklahoma, Texas |
| EPA Region 7<br>726 Minnesota Avenue<br>Kansas City, KS 66101 | Iowa, Kansas, Missouri, Nebraska |

EPA Region 8
999 18th Street
Denver, CO 80202

Colorado, Montana, North Dakota,
South Dakota, Utah, Wyoming

EPA Region 9
75 Hawthorne Street
San Francisco, CA 94105

Arizona, California, Hawaii, Nevada,
American Samoa, Trust Territories
of the Pacific, Guam, Northern
Marianas

EPA Region 10
1200 Sixth Avenue
Seattle, WA 98101

Alaska, Idaho, Oregon, Washington

# APPENDIX D

# Water Purification Equipment Manufacturers

## *Filters*

A.H.P. Inc.
404 East Battlefield
Springfield, MO 65807
(800) 749-2040

Amway (Japan) LTD
Nihon Seimei Minami
  Azabu Building
2-8-12 Minami Azabu
Minato-Ku
Tokyo, 106 JAPAN
(616) 676-6000

Amway Corporation (USA)
7575 East Fulton Road
Ada, MI 49355
(616) 676-6587

Brita Wasser-Filter-System
  GMBH
Heinrich-Hertz Strasse 4
D-65232 Taunusstein-Neuhof
Germany
(49-612) 8872-74

Chemical Engineering Corp.
12628 U.S. 33 N
Churubusco, IN 46723
(219) 693-2141

Culligan International
One Culligan Parkway
Northbrook, IL 60062
(708) 205 6000

Cuno, Inc.
400 Research Parkway
Meriden, CT 06450
(800) 243-6894

Diamite Corp.
1625 McCandless Drive
Milpitas, CA 95035
(408) 945-1001

Doulton Water Filters
5032 Sand Lake Drive
Onstead, MI 49265
(517) 467-4788

Everpure, Inc.
660 N Blackhawk Drive
Westmont, IL 60559
(708) 654-4000

Filtercold Corp.
1840 East University, Suite #2
Tempe, AZ 85281
(602) 894-2941

Hy Cite Corporation
333 Holtzman Road
Madison, WI 53713
(608) 273-3373

Liberty Drinking Water Systems
6702 Bergenline Ave.
West New York, NJ 07093
(201) 662-0351

Multi-Pure Drinking Water
 Systems
21339 Nordhoff Street
Chatsworth, CA 91311
(818) 341-7577

Neo-Life Company of America
3500 Gateway Blvd.
Fremont, CA 94538
(510) 785-0724

Rainsoft Water Conditioning
 Company
2080 E. Lunt Avenue
Elk Grove Village, IL 60007
(708) 437-9400

Regal Ware Inc.
1765 Reigle Drive
Kewaskum, WI 53040
(414) 626-2121

Selecto, Inc.
5933 Peachtree Industrial
 Blvd. #B
Norcross, GA 30092
(800) 635-4017

Teledyne Water Pik
1730 East Prospect Street
Fort Collins, CO 80553-0001
(303) 221-8254

Ultra-Flo Systems
6733 S Sepulveda Blvd.,
 Suite 268
Los Angeles, CA 90045
(310) 337-9248

Water Factory Systems, Inc.
68 Fairbanks
Irvine, CA 92718
(714) 588-1122

Watts Regulator Co.
815 Chestnut Street
North Andover, MA 01845
(508) 688-1811

## *Reverse Osmosis Systems*

Aqua Care Systems
3806 North 29th Avenue
Hollywood, FL 33020
(305) 925-9993

Ecodyne
P.O. Box 64420
St. Paul, MN 55164
(612) 739-5330

Ecowater Systems
P.O. Box 64420
St. Paul, MN 55164
(612) 739-5330

Kinetico, Incorporated
10845 Kinsman Road
P.O. Box 193
Newbury, OH 44065
(216) 564-9111

Kiss International
965 Park Center Drive
Vista, CA 92083-8312
(619) 599-0200

Shaklee Corporation
444 Market Street
San Francisco, CA 94111
(510) 887-5098

The Water Exchange
8210 Wiles Road
Coral Springs, FL 33067
(305) 345-7484

Water Resources International
2800 East Chambers Street
Phoenix, AZ 85040
(800) 788-4420

Watercare Corporation
1520 North 24th Street
Manitowoc, WI 54221-1717
(414) 682-6823

Whirlpool Corporation
2000 M-63
Benton Harbor, MI 49022-2692
(616) 927-7265

Scott Alan Lewis is an environmental writer, policy analyst, and photographer. He has consulted on conservation issues for elected officials, private individuals, and non-profit environmental groups. Scott is a graduate of Colorado College and Stanford Law School. His previous book is *The Rainforest Book*.

Scott lives in Oregon with his wife, Laura, and son, Zachary.